W9-BWX-822

BLACK+DECKER

The best DIY series from the brand you trust

Essential
HOME SKILLS
Handbook

Everything You Need
to Know as a
New Homeowner

CHRIS PETERSON

COOL
SPRINGS
PRESS

Brimming with creative inspiration, how-to projects, and useful information to enrich your everyday life, quarto.com is a favorite destination for those pursuing their interests and passions.

Inspiring | Educating | Creating | Entertaining

© 2022 Quarto Publishing Group USA Inc.

First published in 2022 by Cool Springs Press, an imprint of The Quarto Group,
100 Cummings Center, Suite 265-D,
Beverly, MA 01915, USA.
T (978) 282-9590 F (978) 283-2742 Quarto.com

All rights reserved. No part of this book may be reproduced in any form without written permission of the copyright owners. All images in this book have been reproduced with the knowledge and prior consent of the artists concerned, and no responsibility is accepted by producer, publisher, or printer for any infringement of copyright or otherwise arising from the contents of this publication. Every effort has been made to ensure that credits accurately comply with information supplied. We apologize for any inaccuracies that may have occurred and will resolve inaccurate or missing information in a subsequent reprinting of the book.

Cool Springs Press titles are also available at discount for retail, wholesale, promotional, and bulk purchase. For details, contact the Special Sales Manager by email at specialsales@quarto.com or by mail at The Quarto Group, Attn: Special Sales Manager, 100 Cummings Center, Suite 265-D, Beverly, MA 01915, USA.

26 25 24 23 22   1 2 3 4 5

ISBN: 978-0-7603-7325-5
Digital edition published in 2022
eISBN: 978-0-7603-7326-2

Library of Congress Cataloging-in-Publication Data available

Design: Sylvia McArdle
Cover Image: tk XXXXXXXXXXXXXXXXXXX
Page Layout: Sylvia McArdle
Illustration: Ada Grace
New Photography: Courtesy of BLACK + DECKER: p. 6, 7; Shutterstock: p. 4, 5, 9 (bottom), 11 (bottom left and top right); 14, 16 (top right), 29, 40, 41, 52, 63 (top), 127, 136, 137

Printed in China

The Essential Home Skills Handbook
Created by: The Editors of Cool Springs Press, in cooperation with BLACK+DECKER.
BLACK+DECKER and the BLACK+DECKER logo are trademarks of The Black & Decker Corporation and are used under license. All rights reserved.

NOTICE TO READERS

For safety, use caution, care, and good judgment when following the procedures described in this book. The publisher and BLACK+DECKER cannot assume responsibility for any damage to property or injury to persons as a result of misuse of the information provided.

The techniques shown in this book are general techniques for various applications. In some instances, additional techniques not shown in this book may be required. Always follow manufacturers' instructions included with products, since deviating from the directions may void warranties. The projects in this book vary widely as to skill levels required: Some may not be appropriate for all do-it-yourselfers, and some may require professional help.

Consult your local building department for information on building permits, codes, and other laws as they apply to your project.

Contents

Introduction

This is not just a book. It is an investment that offers handsome returns for any new or inexperienced homeowner. Armed with this reference, any aspiring DIYer can keep his or her house in great shape. This information can reasonably save homeowners hundreds of dollars on repairs they won't need to make, professional charges they avoid, and the increased longevity of expensive fixtures like furnaces and hot water heaters.

Money is just one reward. There is also the immeasurable satisfaction and pride of being master of your own castle. Doing what needs to be done rather than paying a handyman means never worrying about being overcharged or falling victim to substandard work. That control and peace of mind are satisfying bonuses.

A trusted resource close at hand is key for inexperienced homeowners who are often overwhelmed by the demands of a new house (or at least new to you). Fortunately, you are not alone. *The Essential Home Skills Handbook* provides time-tested advice, professional insight, money-saving tips, and guidance you can truly trust. Nobody is born with the skills and knowledge needed to maintain and repair a house. But that knowledge is easy to acquire and useful for a lifetime.

Skills aren't much good without tools, and the beginning craftsperson is only as good as his or her gear. That's why the following pages include a list of basic tools you'll need before you jump into any project. You probably already own most of these, but it's good to make sure you have what you need before tackling any task—especially when mastering important new skills. Projects along the way will sometimes require special tools, but we've kept that to a minimum.

The skills you'll develop in using this book are a foundation to build on. Where turning to a pro makes more sense, you'll find "White Flag" features spelling out how to hire the best professional. "Pro Tips" offer insider advice and shortcuts to make any job easier and quicker. "Money Wise" boxes help you save money.

Before all that, you need to understand the basic structure of a house. All modern residential structures share certain features and standardized components. Learn to work with drywall in one house and you're equipped to tackle it anywhere. Here's a structural overview and where to find critical fixtures and features.

Anatomy of a House

Residential construction starts with the foundation. There are several different types; the best one depends on site geography, local climate, and house structure.

- Post-and-pier. The most basic and least common. Also called "post and beam" or "pile," it consists of concrete piers or screw-type metal piers on which support beams and the house rest. These are used in smaller homes or on unstable soil, such as coastal areas.

Screw piers are more tolerant of ground movement and stress than poured concrete is.

- Crawl space. An option built of short, poured concrete or cinder block walls resting on poured concrete footings. Crawl spaces combine stability with less expense than a full basement. Services can be run under the house.
- Slab. A basic poured-concrete platform. Inexpensive and easy to lay, slabs limit where services such as plumbing can be run. Ground movement can have serious repercussions for a slab foundation.

A slab can support even a large house, but services must be contained elsewhere. Plumbing lines may be placed inside the slab, but that makes future repairs extremely difficult.

- Full basement. Built fully or partially belowground, basements are the most expensive, longest-lasting, and most useful foundations. Poured-concrete walls sit on footings, with a poured-concrete floor. This leaves room for fixtures and services, as well as storage and potentially even a finished living space.

Houses are framed from the foundation up. Some are built of modular, pre-fab sections; but most are constructed with uniform wood structural members such as studs and beams in a process known as "stick framing." Houses are designed to efficiently distribute loads (the weight of structure, occupants, possessions, fixtures, and appliances). The framing serves as the bones, while the "skin" is comprised of weather wrap, siding materials, and the roof structure. These—along with windows and doors—create the "energy envelope." The projects here include common repairs and projects to all those areas. Tackling any of them requires the correct tools.

Safe at Home

Any house contains dangers that can lead to injuries. The good news? Those perils are avoidable; safety is part of learning new skills. Here are general DIY safety guidelines to follow.

- Assume every electrical circuit and fixture is live. Test for current before doing any electrical work, even if you've turned the power off at the breaker box.
- Use the correct tool and keep tools in good working order. Frustration and impatience can lead DIYers to use whatever's at hand. Tools will last longer if you use them only for their intended purposes and clean them after each use.
- Know what you're dealing with before you begin. Not sure whether that bottom layer of paint contains lead or the popcorn ceiling harbors asbestos? Test it or have it tested.
- Never remove safety guards. This is basic common sense, but it's something even experienced DIYers do—and often regret.
- Dress for success. Proper safety gear is not optional. That includes long pants and long-sleeve shirts when dealing with potential skin irritants like fiberglass insulation.
- Know your limits. Attempting to do something for which you are unqualified is a recipe for disaster. Call in a pro when you're overwhelmed. Never attempt a DIY project when you're tired or rushed for time.

The Homeowner's Basic Toolkit

Most home repairs don't call for exotic tools; the most common tools are versatile. Become proficient in using these and you can take on more difficult projects requiring specialized tools. Some projects in this book require the occasional inexpensive and widely available special tool.

Stud finder

Level

Hammer

Tape measure

Screwdriver set

Hand Tools

- **Screwdriver set.** You should have a range of sizes of standard, Phillips head, and Torx (the emerging standard for replacement screws) screwdrivers. All-in-one (a handle with barrel slots containing swap-out heads) "multibit" tools are inexpensive alternatives.

- **Hammer.** A basic claw hammer is essential. Find one that feels good in your hand and is easy to swing given your size and strength (16 ounce is the most common). A rubber grip ensures against slips.

- **Adjustable wrenches.** Useful toolbox additions thanks to adjustability. Buy at least a small and large size but, ideally, a set of three sizes.

- **Tape measure.** Choose one with a durable case and a steel, 25' tape. Lock-out action should be smooth. A laser measuring tool is more precise but pricier and difficult to master, and it won't work in certain circumstances.

- **Levels.** The right level is handy for many different tasks. Purchase a 4' level and a smaller torpedo level.

- **Stud finder.** Pay more for one that is accurate and easy to use. The best not only clearly show stud location; they also indicate wiring and plumbing line locations.

- **Utility knife.** Buy a high-quality utility knife with a fully retractable blade that locks closed, a secure and comfortable handle, and durable outer case.

- **Circuit tester.** Sold as a "neon circuit tester" or "voltage tester," this has two probes—negative and positive. They are held to each side of a circuit; if the bulb lights, voltage is present. This is an essential safety tool for even basic electrical repairs.

- **Pliers.** Purchase a set rather than individual pliers. You should own lineman's, needle-nose, side cutting, and slip-joint pliers. Also buy locking pliers. As the name implies, the adjustable jaws can be locked onto just about any surface.

- **Multipurpose electrician's tool.** This looks like a pair of flat pliers with different size holes in the jaws. It makes stripping and cutting wires easy.

- **Folding worktable or saw horses.** A stable, sturdy portable platform is a must-have. Buy lightweight versions that are easy to break down and transport.

Circular saw

- **Random orbital sander.** A 6" random orbital sander is a middle ground between belt sanders and smaller "palm" sanders. It can quickly smooth a surface while being easy to control. Choose a cordless model.

- **Reciprocating saw.** An all-purpose beast, this can cut through most materials effortlessly. Because the blade projects straight out from the handle, it reaches places other saw blades can't.

Power Tools

Power Drill

- **Power drill.** Pick the most common size for home use—$3/8$". Buy a cordless drill with a backup battery. The best include a carrying case and a drill bit set. Check that the drill is comfortable and doesn't tire your arm.

- **Circular saw.** A "sidewinder" model (motor to the side of the blade) is best for inexperienced DIYers; "worm-drive" models (motor behind the blade) are cumbersome for beginners.

Honorable Mentions

Tool belt

- **Rotary tool.** These tiny but mighty workhorses are sold with a diverse selection of attachments and tips. A fully equipped rotary tool is amazingly versatile.

- **Tool belt and/or tool bucket.** These make it easier to transport the tools you'll need to wherever you'll be using them.

- **Shop vacuum.** A wet/dry vac makes even the messiest project easy and quick to clean up.

Locating Essential Services and Fixtures

Thanks to modern standardized building practices and code requirements, most houses have similar basic service features. Knowing where water and electricity enter your house, where crucial fixtures live, and how to shut everything off is critical in reacting to home breakdowns.

- **Electrical service.** Electricity enters through a buried main line or an overhead "drop line" running from a power pole into a metal service mast sticking out of your roof. In either case, power is routed through the meter on an exterior wall, then into the main breaker (or fuse) box inside. The meter's dial or readout moves or changes when power is flowing. The breaker box holds the main that controls power to the whole house and individual breakers servicing specific areas or rooms. Know where the box is to turn off power for repairs.

- **Water supply and the DWV system.** Water enters most houses from a municipal water main. Some homes are supplied by wells that must be tested and maintained. Know where your water meter or well head are located. Water flows in through a main shutoff valve; locate it so that you can turn it off if there's a leak. Smaller shutoff valves are located on branch feeder lines. Main water valves are usually in a basement or crawl space. Some are underground outside; those are shut off with a special tool. The drain-waste-vent (DWV) system removes water—and wastes—by creating air

Electrical service mast.

Power meter.

A main breaker box. The empty spaces under the breakers are potential new circuits.

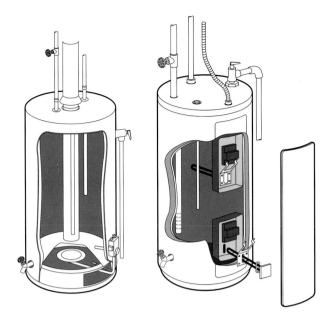

- **pressure that forces everything out the main waste "stack" to a sewer line or septic system.** Municipal sewer systems rarely break down; septic systems are more trouble-prone and require maintenance. Locate the main vertical waste line and cleanout opening. Snaking the cleanout is sometimes the only way to clear a major clog. Know where a septic tank, distribution box, and leach field lie. The tank is accessed for maintenance, and you should never drive over or dig up a leach field.

A water main shutoff valve and water meter.

- **Fire extinguisher.** Ensure there is a fire extinguisher on every level of the house. Everyone in the household should know where extinguishers are and how to use them. Different types are distinguished by letters designating the type of fire the extinguisher addresses: A, B, C, D, and K. D and K extinguishers are not used in the home. A, B, and C are noted with a green triangle, red square, or blue circle, respectively. A treats cloth and paper fires, B extinguishes flammable liquid and grease fires, and C puts out electrical fires. A multipurpose "A, B, C" extinguisher covers all bases.

- **HVAC.** The HVAC (heating, ventilation, and air-conditioning) system keeps a house comfortable year-round and protects indoor air quality. Know the location of your furnace, heat pump, or central air-conditioning condenser. Also check where ductwork is accessible.

- **Water heater.** A water heater serves every faucet, showerhead, and bathtub spout. These hardworking appliances have a limited life span. Any more than twelve years old is well worth replacing; you may be better served by upgrading to newer technology like a tankless heater.

1. Home Heating and Cooling

HVAC stands for heating, ventilation, and air-conditioning. Although those are discreet functions, they are interrelated. A house's HVAC system has a huge impact on money and comfort, as does the home's energy "envelope." The house's skin determines how readily air flows in and out and how outside temperatures impact inside temps. Easy projects, such as installing weather stripping, can significantly lower utility costs and make a house feel less drafty.

A furnace or boiler is the soul of a heating system (the furnace also plays a role in central air-conditioning). Those are expensive mechanicals; maintain them meticulously and make repairs at the first sign of trouble. Regular maintenance extends furnace or central air-conditioning condenser life. Maintenance doesn't require expertise—just knowledge and a willingness to apply it.

HVAC systems impact indoor air quality. The U.S. Environmental Protection Agency reports that indoor air is, on average, two to five times more polluted than outside air. Proper ventilation, and regularly replacing heating and cooling filters, keeps a house healthier.

How HVAC Works

HVAC systems draw clean outside air inside and exhaust indoor air polluted with cooking odors, dust, airborne microbes, and more. Your HVAC system heats or cools air before distributing it. Air movement can also be passive, flowing in through windows, doors, cracks, and holes.

HVAC Types

All HVAC systems are either *single-stage* or *zoned*. Single-stage systems heat (or cool) the whole house. Zoned systems offer more control and economy because heating and cooling can be limited to specific areas. The systems below are the most common.

- **Forced-air:** The most common system, a furnace draws outside air in through a blower, heats it, and pushes it into ductwork feeding vents throughout the house. The air passes through a filter before distribution. Blowers also distribute cooled air from a central air condenser unit.

- **Steam/hot water:** Water is heated in a boiler, then steam or hot water is distributed to radiators in each room. Controlling temperature in a given room is harder than with a forced-air system, and leaks pose a serious problem.

- **Electric and radiant:** Electric heating is generally limited to temperate regions because it is relatively expensive. Electricity heats coils in baseboard units, which can be shut off to save money. Radiant systems use coils under flooring for room-by-room solutions.

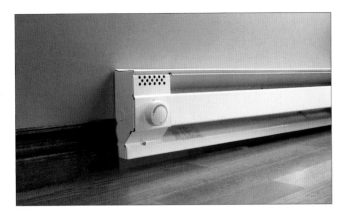

Air-Conditioning

Some air-conditioning overlaps with heating systems. Local cooling solutions are independent. Other technologies, such as swamp coolers, are rare.

- **Central air-conditioning:** An exterior condenser unit pulls warm air over coils containing refrigerant that draws heat from the air rather than actually cooling it (a difference without a distinction for homeowners). The cooled air is drawn into the furnace blower. It passes over an evaporator that eliminates and drains off moisture. The blower distributes the cooled, dry air throughout the house.

- **Ductless:** Also called "mini-split" systems, these are a relatively recent innovation. A wall unit piped to a smaller-than-normal outside condenser services each room. Air is cooled, drawn in, and blown out of the unit, which can also heat air. This is a zone solution, so you only pay to heat or cool rooms you're using.

- **Localized:** Window or wall-sleeve units serve a single room well. These are awkward to set up, and capacity has to be correctly matched to the space to avoid excess energy costs. But they are quick and easy solutions.

The Special Case of Heat Pumps

Unlike furnaces, heat pumps don't generate heat. They pull heat from air either inside or outside the house—depending on whether the pump is cooling or heating—moving it to the opposite side of the system. For heating, refrigerant-filled exterior pump coils draw heat even from cold air, transferring that heat inside through the interior coil unit. The process is reversed for cooling. Heat pumps can be air-based or geothermal—pulling heat from underground.

Home Ventilation

Stale air must be constantly exhausted and replaced by clean outside air to maintain healthy indoor air quality. This happens through soffit and gable vents, windows, and doors. Air is also exhausted locally, such as with a bathroom fan. An attic or roof whole-house fan creates wind chill that cools the interior while pulling air through the house. Unintended air leakage happens through gaps around wall openings for pipes and conduit. These openings can represent significant loss, and plugging them saves money.

Install V-Strip Door Weather Stripping

TIME: 15 minutes / **SKILL LEVEL:** Easy

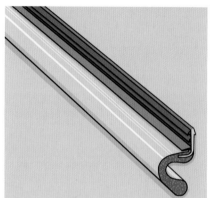

Weather stripping lowers energy bills and increases home comfort. There are several types, but all physically block gaps along window and door edges while allowing the structures to open and close as intended.

- **Adhesive-backed:** The simplest, cheapest, and least effective. This is foam or tubular vinyl with adhesive on one side. The weather stripping is cut and stuck on the bottom and jambs of windows and doors. It compresses over time and with use, rarely lasting more than two years.

- **Nail-on/screw-on:** Durable and effective, this is nailed or screwed onto windows and doors. Hard metal weather stripping can only be used for uniform, rather than irregular, gaps. Vinyl or rubber versions are better for irregular gaps. This type wears out over time and is harder to replace than self-adhesive versions.

- **V-strip:** This is used on doors with an existing channel ("kerf") between door stop and jamb. Made of rubber, vinyl, or similar material, V-strip has a mounting tab attached to a bumper. Sold in standard lengths, it is cut to fit and pressed into place. When the door is closed, the bumper compresses and blocks airflow. Easy to install, inexpensive, and effective, V-strip is ideal if the door construction has the necessary kerf.

- **Rope caulk:** Used in older homes in colder regions, rope caulk is a quick and easy—if unattractive—way to seal gaps around windows that won't be opened over winter. The caulk blocks airflow and is easily peeled off in spring.

- **Door sweeps:** Exterior door-bottom gaps are a main source of un pleasant drafts. Most weather stripping would cause the door to stick, but door "sweeps" eliminate this problem. The simplest are metal or rubber strips fastened to the interior bottom door edge, with bristles or a rubber curtain hanging down. "Cap" sweeps have a U profile and bristles on the bottom. The cap is glued or screwed onto the door bottom.

What You'll Need

- 120" × 1" vinyl-clad foam kerf door seal
- Lineman's pliers
- All-purpose cleaner and rag
- Tape measure
- Heavy-duty scissors or utility knife

How You Do It

1. Grab the existing kerf door seal with lineman's pliers and remove it. Clean the frame all around. Repair rotted wood or other defects.

2. Measure and cut weather stripping sections to fit. Trim one end of each long side piece (both ends of the top piece) to a 45° angle, for the corners. *Optional:* Alternatively, install the piece as purchased (usually sold in 81" lengths) and trim the opposite end.

3. Starting from the bottom of one side jamb, press one end of the tongue into the jamb gap. Continue pressing the weather stripping in place all the way up. Repeat with the top piece, then the opposite side. Check that the door closes securely.

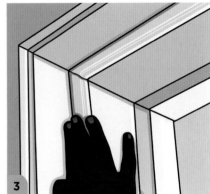

Install Peel-and-Stick Weather Stripping

TIME: 10 minutes / **SKILL LEVEL:** Easy

Pick a product wide enough for the window bottom and thick enough to completely seal your gaps.

What You'll Need

- All-purpose cleaner
- Rag
- Putty knife
- Tape measure
- Self-adhesive weather stripping
- Scissors

How You Do It

1. Inspect the sash and jamb for defects. Repair any before continuing. Clean the window edge and jamb where the weather stripping will stick when the window is closed. Use a putty knife to remove any buildup.

2. Measure the window bottom. Cut the weather stripping to length using scissors.

3. Remove the protective tape and press the weather stripping onto the edge, pushing hard for 15 seconds to ensure a tight bond. Check that the window closes securely.

Apply Window Film

TIME: 40 minutes / **SKILL LEVEL:** Moderate

Window film is a micro-thin layer of either polyester or vinyl. Some versions are translucent, while others are opaque; all are sold in rolls 36" or 48" wide. The one used here is energy-conserving temperature-control film. Others offer different benefits, such as privacy. Regardless, patience is the most important tool in applying window film. Be careful and keep an eye on details (especially cleaning the window and frame thoroughly). Done correctly, it is almost impossible to tell the film is in place.

Temperature-control film

Privacy film

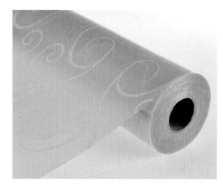

Decorative film

What You'll Need

- Window cleaner
- Lint-free clean cloths
- Tape measure (optional)
- Scissors
- Spray bottle
- Baby shampoo
- Window scraper
- Sponge
- Window squeegee
- Painter's tape
- Smoothie squeegee (or similar)
- Five-way tool (or similar straightedge)
- Utility knife with new blade

- **Temperature-control film:** Formulated to stop heat and cold from transferring through glass, this type is available clear or tinted. Tinted films block harmful UV rays and can prevent furniture upholstery from fading. Some are meant for summer, while "four-season" products keep the interior warm or cool, depending on the season.

- **Privacy film:** This film has a reflective side that is installed facing out, blocking the view into the home. Used on windows or doors, some block UV rays. These can, however, make it difficult to see out at certain times.

- **Decorative film:** Decorative film creates the appearance of frosted, textured, or stained glass. The pricier the product, the more convincing the illusion. These are ideal for bathrooms or other private areas. Some also block UV rays.

- **Security film:** Security film makes it harder to shatter a window and keeps broken glass from scattering. The thick film can stop thieves from gaining access through a broken window or glass door.

Some films can be removed and reused, although that's laborious. Most homeowners consider the film permanent once installed. Warranty coverage and length are signs of quality. Budget films are subject to scratches, bubbling, and fading. Window films sold through home centers can be purchased with all-in-one application kits. The steps remain the same, but read and follow the manufacturer's directions.

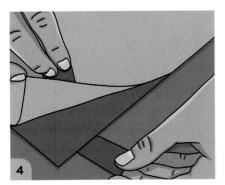

How You Do It

1. Only install film out of direct sunlight. Clean the window thoroughly. Measure and cut the film 1" larger than the window all around. The cutting surface must be absolutely clean to ensure against tears or dirt. *Pro Tip:* Rather than cut on a table, wet the glass and unroll the film over it (it will stick). Use scissors to cut the film about 1" larger all around. Stick the cut panel onto a nearby window to keep it safe and ready for installation.

2. Fill a spray bottle with cool water and a teaspoon of baby shampoo. Spray the window. Scrape it with a window scraper, in horizontal rows, top to bottom. This removes small, stuck bits, or old paint drops.

3. Spray the window and use a sponge to scrub the glass. Wipe with a squeegee, clearing the blade with a clean, lint-free cloth after each pass. Wipe down the frame's inside edges.

4. Determine the film's liner side (usually the slicker side or paper layer—check the instructions). Stick a tab of painter's tape on each side and carefully pull liner and film apart.

5. Spray the cut panel and the window center with the shampoo mix. Center the panel on the window. Smooth from the center out with a smoothie squeegee—or whatever tool the manufacturer recommends. Stop 1" short of edges to avoid pushing the film into the joint.

6. Use a five-way tool or similar straightedge to press the film into the top corner of the window. Carefully slice the film along the inside of the straightedge using a utility knife fit with a new blade.

7. Carefully move the straightedge down the frame, keeping the utility knife blade alongside the straightedge and slicing as you go. Repeat the process at the top, other side, and bottom.

8. Wet the panel and use the smoothie squeegee to squeeze remaining water out from under the film. Work from the center out to the edges. Absorb water with a clean, lint-free cloth.

Pro Tip

Some manufacturers and instructions call for cutting film along the frame's inner edges. Instead, leave a $\frac{1}{16}$" gap for water to be pressed out during your final squeegee, preventing water from wicking back under the film. The gap also allows film to expand and contract without wrinkling.

Insulate an Attic

TIME: 1 hour / **SKILL LEVEL:** Easy

Hot air rises, making the attic and roof avenues for heat escape. Insulation keeps that heat inside a home's living areas, and a properly insulated attic lowers energy bills. Insulating an attic must be done correctly to be effective. That starts with the correct materials.

Insulation is rated by the "R-value"—how resistant the material is to heat flow. R-values are standardized to 1 square inch of material. So, for example, an R-value of 3.2 translates to an overall R-value of 19.2 if 6" of material is used. For an unfinished attic, the Department of Energy recommends R-30 in southern regions such as Georgia; R-38 in moderate regions such as Kansas; and R-49 in cold northern regions such as Vermont.

Beyond R-value, there are two insulating methods: blown-in "loose" fill (fiberglass, cellulose, or mineral wool) or "batts" (fiberglass or mineral wool), which are cut and layered. Blown-in attic insulation requires getting a blower up to an inconvenient space. Consequently, this project describes installing batts, the more common DIY option. Batts come in rolls and precut sections. Precut batts are more expensive but easier and more convenient for standard sized, open joist spaces. Rolls are better for odd shapes and sizes of openings.

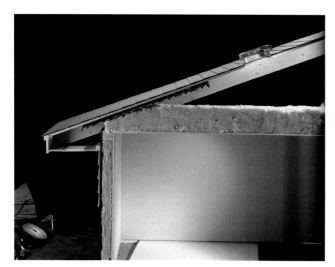

Unfaced batting between attic joists must leave room for proper attic ventilation.

Insulation Types

- **Fiberglass:** The most common home insulation material, available loose and as batts. Spun glass fibers create air pockets that slow heat transfer.

Faced fiberglass batts must always be installed with the facing correctly oriented to avoid moisture problems.

Cellulose

- **Cellulose:** Only available as loose fill, cellulose is made from recycled newspapers and wood waste. Considered environmentally friendly, the "green" credibility is undercut for insulation treated with fire retardant (required prior to attic use).

- **Mineral wool:** Made from recycled slag and melted stone spun into fibers, mineral wool is gaining in popularity. It's available loose or as batts and installed in the same way fiberglass is.

Safe at Home

Houses constructed before 1990 may have blown-in attic insulation containing vermiculite (apparent as shiny flecks). This may contain dangerous asbestos. Have the insulation tested and don't disturb it. You can leave vermiculite insulation if it will never be disturbed. However, if you're upgrading insulation or want to increase resale value, have the insulation removed by a licensed contractor certified in asbestos abatement, handling, and disposal.

3

4

Optional

What You'll Need

- Tape measure
- Fiberglass insulation rolls or precut batts
- Safety glasses
- Dust mask
- Heavy-duty work gloves
- Fire-resistant caulk
- Caulk gun
- Fire-resistant expanding spray foam
- Utility knife with new blade
- Waste 2×4
- Long metal straightedge
- Prefab rafter baffles (optional)
- Staple gun (optional)
- Foam board insulation (optional)
- Construction adhesive (optional)

How You Do It

1. Measure the rafter space to determine amount of material you'll need (including any top layer to create the desired R-value). Purchase the insulation, adding 10 percent for waste. Buy faced (paper on one side) insulation only for the bottom layer of currently uninsulated joist spaces. Wear a long-sleeve shirt, long pants, and durable closed-toe shoes or boots. Put on a dust mask, safety glasses, and puncture-resistant gloves.

2. Seal around electrical boxes in joist cavities, using fire-resistant caulk. Use expanding foam in gaps wider than ¼". Check labels on recessed lighting fixtures; any labeled "IC"—insulation contact—can be covered with batts. Otherwise, box out fixtures with cardboard or wood to maintain at least a 3" space all around the fixture. The same is true of metal vent flues.

3. Measure joist cavity length and width (leaving a gap at the soffit for airflow). Cut batting to size with a utility knife, kneeling on a waste 2×4 and using it as a straightedge for crosscuts (width), or using a long metal straightedge for rip (length) cuts. *Optional:* To ensure insulation doesn't move and block soffit vents, staple or tape polystyrene foam (such as Styrofoam) or plastic rafter baffles in rafter cavities, over soffits.

4. Lay batts in place. Use faced batting only on the first, bottom layer, with the paper facing down. Cut and lay unfaced batts on top to build up R-value, until the insulation is level with the top of joists. To increase R-value, add a layer of batting perpendicular to the joists. *Optional:* Insulate the attic-hatch opening. There are several ways to do this. Cut layers of foam board insulation to size, gluing each layer to the one under and above it. This creates a block that rests on the opening's stops. For common pull-down stairs, use a utility knife to cut sides for a topless box of board insulation. The inside dimensions should be just larger than the pull-down ladder dimensions. Glue the sides together with solvent-free construction adhesive.

Pro Tip

These steps describe insulating joist cavities. If you plan on finishing the attic, insulate rafter cavities. Install baffles between rafters to maintain airflow. Cut batts precisely; they must be wide enough to hold once pushed in place, until the drywall is installed. The final layer should be faced insulation, with the paper facing the interior.

Seal Energy Envelope Air Leaks

TIME: 30 minutes / **SKILL LEVEL:** Easy

HVAC ventilation is all about controlling when and where air flows. Leaks waste money, make the home less comfortable, and make the HVAC system less efficient. They are also access for pests. Check any service that enters through a wall, including pipes, conduit, or wiring. Sealing a leak depends on the opening's size.

What You'll Need

- Screwdriver
- Outlet and light switch gaskets
- Caulk gun
- Exterior and interior paintable caulk sealant (or substitute an indoor/outdoor sealant caulk)
- Utility knife or putty knife
- Spray insulating foam sealant

How You Do It

1. Remove exterior-wall electrical outlet cover plates. Slip an insulating gasket over each receptacle. Screw down the cover plate tight enough to compress the gasket. Repeat with exterior-wall light switches.

2. Caulk gaps less than 1/4" wide around exterior wall electrical boxes with acrylic latex sealant caulk. Unscrew the faceplate. Cut off the cartridge tip with a utility knife. Secure the cartridge in a caulk gun and apply a steady, even bead between box and drywall. Smooth the bead with a moistened fingertip.

3. Remove bathroom vent fan covers and caulk gaps less than 1/4" between the fan unit and drywall. Caulk around electrical box openings and vertical vent stacks in an unfinished attic. Fill any gaps greater than 1/4" with expanding foam sealant meant for interior use.

4. Caulk around exterior vent hoods, such as over the dryer vent, using exterior-grade caulk. Fill gaps around exterior pipes or conduits, or holes in exterior walls that can't be accessed from the inside, with exterior-grade expanding foam sealant.

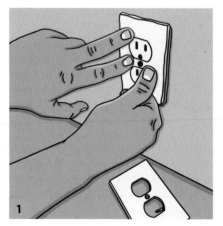

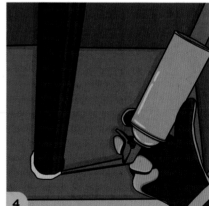

Insulate a Crawl Space

TIME: 1 hour / **SKILL LEVEL:** Moderate

Even in professional circles there is disagreement about how best to insulate crawl space. Decades ago, standard practice was to insulate between joists, leaving airflow through sidewall vents. Current thinking is that this promotes moisture conditions that can lead to mold, rot, and termite infestation. The steps below describe insulating the sidewalls, blocking vents, and laying a ground vapor barrier. This extends the energy envelope of the room above. (Some pros advocate also insulating joist cavities.) In any case, consult a reputable local HVAC professional for an up-to-date recommendation.

What You'll Need

- Dust mask
- Heavy-duty work gloves
- Eye protection
- Tape measure
- 1½" foam board insulation
- Utility knife
- Construction adhesive (solvent-free)
- 6-mil plastic sheeting
- Scissors
- Acrylic vapor barrier tape
- Prefab vent covers or custom plywood covers (optional)

How You Do It

1. Seal leaks and fix existing moisture problems. Remove debris and any tattered insulation in joist cavities. Measure and cut the first board insulation panel.

2. Apply solvent-free construction adhesive to the insulation panel. Hold it in place for about 30 seconds, or until the bond is secure. Cut and install the remaining panels. Cut smaller sections to fill any rim joist cavities. Check that each piece fits before cutting the next.

3. Spread 6-mil plastic sheeting over the ground, running 4" to 6" up each wall. Cut it with scissors and tape it to the walls with acrylic tape. Overlap sheets by 4", taping all seams. *Optional:* If you will regularly access the crawl space, use stakes to secure sheets in place.

4. Install prefab vent covers over any crawl space vents. As an alternative, fabricate plywood covers.

Caulk Window and Door Trim

TIME: 20–40 minutes (depending on number of doors and windows) / **SKILL LEVEL:** Easy

Window and door trim gaps visually disappear into siding, but they are HVAC weak spots. The gaps open during expansion and contraction; even if they have been caulked, the caulk deteriorates over time. Recaulking ensures an airtight seal. It's simple, but laying a tidy caulk bead requires practice. Spend more for a caulk gun with a thumb release, which provides greater control (allowing you to stop flow as desired). Follow these guidelines for laying the perfect bead:

- Cut less off the tip than you think necessary; you can always cut more, but you can't add back.
- Use one hand on the barrel and the other to control flow. The barrel hand should be held near the nozzle.
- Move steadily. Rushing is the number one cause of unattractive caulk beads.
- Find the best wrist position and don't change. For vertical seams, this means bending at the knees as you move down.
- Slide the tube nozzle along the smoothest surface to avoid bead imperfections.
- Tape off seam sides with painter's tape if you are not confident in laying a uniform bead freehand.

What You'll Need

- Drop cloth
- Caulk finishing kit with remover and finisher tools (or substitute a putty knife and your finger)
- Caulk gun with thumb release
- Caulk
- Utility knife
- Painter's tape (optional)
- Caulk finishing tool (optional)

Money Wise

Check caulk tube labels. Caulk for bathrooms is specially formulated for wet and humid environments. For interior door trim, use a paintable latex caulk. Use an exterior-grade caulk (labeled "doors, windows, and siding") on exterior trim. Exterior window or door trim set into masonry calls for special masonry caulk.

How You Do It

1. Place a drop cloth under interior trim. Use a putty knife or caulk removal tool to remove any old caulk, flaking paint, or other debris from the seams.

2. Cut off the tip of the tube with utility knife or the cutter in the gun handle. Put the tube in the gun and begin laying the bead. (To protect nearby surfaces from caulk, you may wish to trim the area with painter's tape.) If you're having trouble maintaining a steady, even bead, stop in the center and begin again from the opposite end into the center.

3. Smooth the bead with a wet fingertip or a caulk finishing tool. Repeat the process with the remaining seams, inside and out.

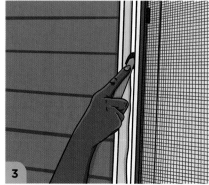

Install Battery-Operated Carbon Monoxide and Smoke Detectors

TIME: 15 minutes (per detector) / **SKILL LEVEL:** Easy

Fire and carbon monoxide are dangers in any house. Fire spreads amazingly fast. Burning plastics and other substances produce toxic gases. Carbon monoxide is even more deadly because it is odorless and colorless. That's why detectors for both are essential. You can buy combination detectors, but check local codes before you do. Many require new detectors be hardwired and equipped with battery backups. Some circumstances and locations, however, require battery-powered detectors. For instance, locating one where there isn't an accessible circuit into which you can tap.

You'll choose between *ionization* and *photoelectric* fire detectors. Ionization types see flames more quickly; photoelectric is faster to detect smoke. Pay a bit more for detectors that include both, or use ionization near features like fireplaces where fires might start, and photoelectric near bedrooms, where smoke will be the first sign of danger. Install detectors inside each bedroom and in hallways within 10' of any bedroom. Mount a detector in any common living area, on each level of the home, and in stairways.

What You'll Need

- Smoke and carbon monoxide detectors
- Tape measure
- Pencil
- Power drill and bits
- Wood or polyurethane mallet (optional)

How You Do It

1. Measure and mark detector location on ceiling; it must be at least 6" from any wall. Use the detector's mounting bracket as a template to mark mounting holes.

2. Drill pilot holes at the marks using the bit specified by the manufacturer. Drill a screw-type anchor into the holes. Some manufacturers provide "push-in" anchors (if you drilled into a joist, you only need a screw). Drill a larger hole and push or tap the anchor in. Use the mounting hardware that came with the detector.

3. Screw the mounting plate to the ceiling using the supplied screws. Put batteries in the detector and attach it to the mounting plate (usually twist and lock). Test the detector. Clean the unit regularly with a clean, lint-free cloth. Change the batteries twice a year.

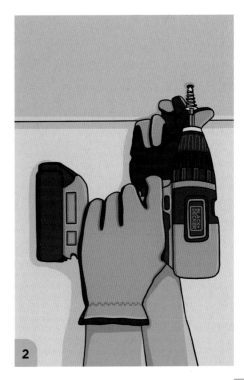

2

● ● ●

Hardwire Carbon Monoxide and Smoke Detectors

TIME: 45 minutes / **SKILL LEVEL:** Challenging

Many homeowners choose to have a licensed electrician install detectors; a pro works faster (and many people are leery of electricity). You can also contract a local licensed electrician to check your work and ensure everything is safe and to code.

What You'll Need

- Smoke and carbon monoxide detectors
- Self-clamping PVC ceiling electrical outlet box ("old work" box)
- Stud finder
- Power drill and bits
- Flex bit auger (optional)
- Tape measure
- Pencil
- Drywall saw
- Circuit tester
- Fish tape
- Combination tool
- 14-gauge NM cable
- Wire connectors
- Screwdriver

How You Do It

1. Measure and mark detector locations. Start with the unit closest to the circuit you'll be tapping into (labeled in the breaker box—see page 8). Locate detectors at least 6" from any walls.

2. Use a stud finder to locate and mark joist locations (you may need to adjust detector location to install the electrical box between joists). *Optional:* If you're mounting the detector below an unfinished attic, drill a hole with a flex bit auger (long, thin specialty bit). Check the attic for where the auger came through to ensure there are no obstructions. This also reveals where you'll need to remove attic floorboards—a necessity in some cases.

3. Use the electrical box to mark the ceiling cutout. Drill a large access hole inside the circle and cut it out with a drywall saw.

4. Turn the power off to the circuit at the breaker box. Test with a circuit tester to ensure it's off and splice NM cable into the circuit. Use fish tape to pull the cable to the detector location and into the new electrical box through the punch-out. (If you're wiring detectors in a series, route NM cable from the box to the next one.)

5. Clamp the box in place by screwing the wings open against the dry wall. Screw the detector mounting base to the box.

6. Wire the detector (in and out, if in a series) with red to red or orange, black to black, and white to white, using the appropriate size wire connectors (see page 103). Wire the ground wire to the detector's ground if it has one or to the incoming and outgoing cable ground (cap with a wire connector if not using). Twist the detector onto the base plate and, once all detectors are installed, test each.

2

3

6

Replace a Bathroom Fan

TIME: 1 hour / **SKILL LEVEL:** Challenging

Bathroom fan technology is increasingly more efficient and quieter. If your fan is more than fifteen years old or is noisy and ineffective, it's time to upgrade. Buy a fan according to the CFM (cubic foot per minute) rating—how much air the fan moves through the space each minute—and the Sones, or loudness rating. Measure the room and use the manufacturer's guidelines to match the fan's rated CFM to the cubic footage. A Sones of 2 is average and considered "quiet."

What You'll Need

- Exhaust fan
- Circuit tester
- Standard screwdriver
- Combination tool
- Drywall saw (optional)
- Oscillating saw (optional)
- 2×4 blocking (optional)
- Power drill and bits (optional)
- 2 ½" deck screws (optional)
- Wire nuts

How You Do It

1. Check that the existing fan exhausts through an exterior wall or, in the case of a top-floor bathroom, a gable or roof vent. If not, add ductwork and a vent. That's a big job best left to a licensed pro (but see the following project to learn how it's done).

2. Turn off the power at the breaker box. Remove the fan cover and use a circuit tester on the motor relay to check that power is off.

3. Remove the fan from its housing. The motor is usually screwed to the housing; unscrew or disassemble any attachments.

4. Disconnect the wires (directly wired motors are unscrewed from the terminals; others unplug from the housing; the housing is disconnected by removing the wire connectors).

5. Unscrew the housing from the joists or use an oscillating saw to cut any attachments. Once unattached, manipulate the housing and remove it.

6. Check that the new fan will fit through the existing hole. If not, adjust the opening with a drywall saw. Consult the manufacturer's instructions for mounting. Add blocking as needed to extend the joist face for mounting the new fan. (Most fans come with screw-type expandable joist brackets.)

7. Connect the wires to the fan and install the housing to the joists or brackets. Install the fan unit in the housing if they are separate and replace the cover. Turn the power on and test the fan.

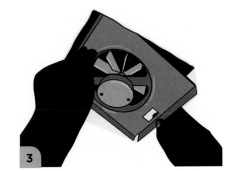

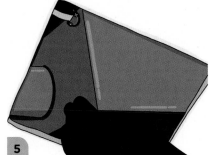

● ● ●

Vent a Bathroom Exhaust Fan through the Attic

TIME: 2 hours / **SKILL LEVEL:** Challenging

Top-floor bathrooms in older homes are often exhausted directly into the attic. This can cause mold and rot. It's wise (and mandated by most codes) to vent through the roof. If you're not comfortable working on a roof, call an HVAC pro. In any case, it helps to know how the fan is supposed to be exhausted.

How You Do It

1. Remove insulation around the fan to access the exhaust port. If the fan has an integral heater, install blocking to keep insulation away from the unit. Mark the heater location in case you need to move it during this process.

2. Mark the exhaust tailpiece exit location on the underside of the roof sheathing. Drill a pilot hole for saw blade access and use an oscillating saw to cut through the sheathing and roofing.

3. Remove enough shingles around the cutout to accommodate the vent flange, leaving the tar paper intact.

4. Secure the exhaust tailpiece through the cutout by screwing down the flange or use a hose clamp if the manufacturer's instructions recommend it. Attach the exhaust duct over the tailpiece. Slide the duct's opposite end onto the fan's exhaust outlet. Slip hose clamps or straps around each end of the duct and tighten the clamps. Wrap the duct with pipe insulation.

5. Coat the bottom of the vent hood with roofing cement and slide the hood over the tailpiece's outside end. Nail the hood flange to the roof. Coat the flange with roofing cement and replace the shingles, cut to fit over the flange.

What You'll Need

- 2×6 blocking (optional)
- Power drill and bits
- Oscillating saw
- Screwdriver
- (2) 4" hose clamps or straps
- Pipe insulation
- Roofing cement
- Roofing nails
- Hammer

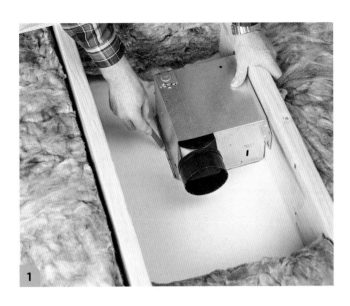

Clean and Maintain Central Air-Conditioning

TIME: 20 minutes / **SKILL LEVEL:** Easy

Central air-conditioning is an expensive luxury, so it only makes sense to maintain the equipment. A little effort heads off costly repairs and extends condenser and evaporator longevity.

What You'll Need

- Crescent wrench or screwdriver
- Shop vacuum
- Spray-on coil cleaner
- Soft-bristle brush
- Fin repair tool
- Canned compressed air

How You Do It

1. Switch off the power at the breaker box and the unit's main breaker. Check the air lines to and from the condenser. Replace damaged insulation.

2. Clean off the condenser's exterior. Unbolt or unscrew the fan cage and lift the fan out. Use a shop vacuum to remove any debris from inside. If you don't have a shop vacuum, clean out by hand.

3. Use a hose with a spray nozzle to spray debris out from between the condenser fins, working from the inside. If stubborn gunk is stuck to the fins, use a spray-on coil cleaner and a soft brush to scrub it off.

4. Use a fin comb to carefully straighten bent fins. This tool is inexpensive; choose one with multiple heads for different size fins.

5. Unfasten the access panel right before the furnace blower inside the house. Use canned compressed air to blow debris off the air conditioner evaporator coils. Spray with a foaming coil cleaner and follow the label directions to clean the evaporator.

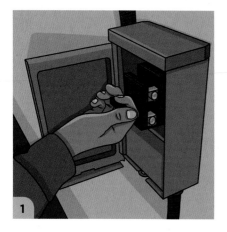

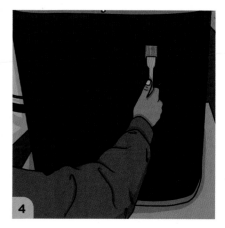

Clean an Evaporator Condensate Drain Line

TIME: 15 minutes / **SKILL LEVEL:** Easy

A blocked evaporator drain line can lead to mold buildup and flooding. The drain removes condensation resulting from warm air passing over cool evaporator coils. The moisture drips into a pan and is routed to a basement drain or directly outside.

What You'll Need

- Shop vacuum
- Rags
- White vinegar

How You Do It

1. Turn air-conditioning off, and turn off power to the furnace at the breaker box. Remove the air filter. Remove the access panel, if there is one, so that you have access to the evaporator pan and drain line.

2. Soak up standing water. Remove a blockage by locating the drain line outlet. Place the wet/dry vac hose mouth over the opening and seal around it with a wet rag. Turn on the vacuum and suck the clog out. (If this doesn't clear the line, snake it.)

3. Clean the drain line by slowly pouring a half-and-half solution of warm water and vinegar into the drain. Wait 20 minutes and flush the line with hot water.

Clean and Maintain Ductless Air-Conditioning

TIME: 30 minutes / **SKILL LEVEL:** Easy

Ductless air-conditioning—also called "mini-splits"—is a room-by-room system. This reduces energy costs and gives you more control. Ductless systems require regular maintenance and cleaning, which will extend the life of the equipment.

What You'll Need

- Spray-on coil and fin cleaner
- Soft-bristle brush
- Rags
- Dish soap
- All-purpose household cleaner

How You Do It

1. Turn off the wall unit and switch off power at the breaker box (for both the room and condenser). Switch on the wall unit to test that no power is going to the condenser. Inspect the condenser and make sure there is at least 4' of clearance all around. Brush off loose debris with soft-bristle brush or rag.

2. Saturate the fins and coil with spray-on coil and fin cleaner. Let stand for 10 minutes. Spray off using a hose with spray attachment.

3. Open the wall unit's cover. Remove the end of the filter from behind the tabs and slide the filter out. Repeat with the second filter if there is one.

4. Gently wash the filters with a mild solution of warm water and dish soap. Rinse thoroughly and let air-dry. Use a clean, lint-free cloth to wipe dirt or debris from the fins behind the filters. Clean the unit with a mild all-purpose cleaner.

5. Slip the dry filters into their channels and secure behind the tabs. Close the unit and turn the power on. If it's been more than six months, change the batteries in the remote.

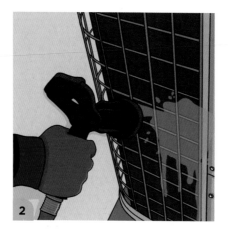

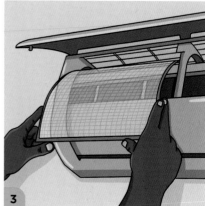

Replace a Furnace Filter

TIME: 5 minutes / **SKILL LEVEL:** Easy

Your furnace filter defends against indoor air contaminants. Replace it every four to six weeks—more or less frequently based on local conditions and how much use the HVAC system sees.

Money Wise

Bargain filters are not necessarily economical because they clog more quickly and block fewer contaminants. Here are the replacement options.

- **Fiberglass:** A synthetic-fiber screen trapped on front and back between cardboard or plastic grids, these capture larger particulates.

- **Pleated paper:** The next step up, this filter is just as it sounds—a thick, pleated-paper sheet contained inside a cardboard frame.

- **Reusable electrostatic:** Similar to metal range hood filters, these are made with metal faces and frames and trap fine particulates that might pass through other filters. They are expensive but reusable—pull out the filter, wash it, and reinstall. The higher initial cost is amortized over time.

- **HEPA:** High-efficiency particulate air (HEPA) filters are treated to catch allergens and even microbes. They are worth the significant expense for anyone with severe respiratory issues or a compromised immune system.

Save more by purchasing filters in bulk. Remove one side of the box to expose filter edges, and mark them with the dates they should be installed.

How You Do It

1. Turn off the power to the furnace at the breaker box. Locate the access panel (positioned horizontally or vertically right before the blower intake) and remove it.

2. Note the arrow direction on the filter's edge. The new filter must point the same direction (direction doesn't matter for reusable filters). Remove and discard the filter.

3. Replace it with the same or better quality. Match the new filter dimensions to the old. Slide the new filter into place and reposition the access panel. Turn the power back on.

Install a Thermostatic Radiator Valve

TIME: 25 minutes / **SKILL LEVEL:** Moderate

Hot-water radiators in older homes experience many issues, but the most frustrating is lack of control. One room is stifling hot, while another is too cool. The answer is a thermostatic radiator valve (TRV). The valve controls the flow of hot water into a radiator. Even if radiators have TRVs, it's worth upgrading to a newer version for greater control. Replacing or installing one isn't difficult but requires a couple unusual tools. However, retrofitting a house full of old radiators makes buying those tools a good investment (and they're handy for future plumbing repairs).

What You'll Need

- Pipe wrenches
- Spud wrench
- Pipe thread sealant
- TRV valve
- Power drill and bits (optional, for mounting)
- Screwdriver (optional, for mounting)

How You Do It

1. Turn off the heat. Close the radiator's water shutoff valve. Drain the radiator. Use a large pipe wrench to loosen the large union nut connecting the tailpiece to the current valve. Use the wrench to loosen the nut between the nipple (the vertical piece running into the floor) and the TRV; use a second wrench to hold the nipple.

2. Unscrew the existing valve and remove. Use a spud wrench and pipe wrench to remove the spud from the radiator inlet.

3. Coat the new spud's threads with pipe thread sealant. Use the spud wrench and pipe wrench to tighten the new spud onto the radiator. Coat the nipple threads with pipe thread sealant. Tighten the new TRV valve onto the nipple (don't overtighten) and finish with the outlet facing the radiator.

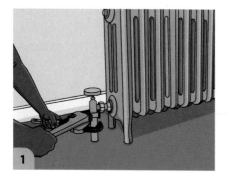

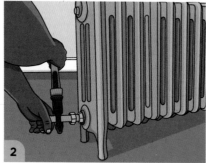

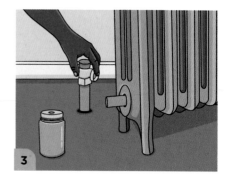

4. Dab the spud with pipe thread sealant and line up the TRV outlet with the radiator inlet. Use a pipe wrench to tighten the union nut to make the connection.

5. Some TRVs have an integral sensor and control. Others are wired to separate controls mounted on a nearby surface. If your TRV has a separate control, decide where you'll mount it. Use the supplied hardware to attach the control (usually screwing the control body to the surface and fastening a faceplate over it). Route the sensor wire where it will be as inconspicuous as possible and screw the sensor control unit onto the TRV.

Replace a Steam-Heat Radiator Air Vent

TIME: 5 minutes / **SKILL LEVEL:** Easy

Old cast-iron radiators are typically equipped with an air vent that bleeds off excess air in the system. These are prone to failure.

What You'll Need

- Radiator air vent
- Thread seal tape, such as Teflon tape
- Rag
- Lubricating spray solvent

How You Do It

1. Turn off the heat and let the radiator cool. Wrap the new vent's threaded stem with seal tape.

2. Use a rag to grip the existing air vent and steadily turn it counterclockwise. Do not force it. Instead, spray the threads with a lubricating spray solvent, let it soak, and then unscrew the vent.

3. Screw the new air vent into the radiator, turning clockwise. Hand tighten, finishing with the vent pointing upward.

Quiet Hot-Water Heating Pipes

TIME: 15 minutes / **SKILL LEVEL:** Easy

Hot-water pipes banging is annoying. It may seem mysterious but is just physics. Metal pipes cool and contract overnight. As heated water begins to flow in the morning, pipes heat and expand, knocking against the wood members to which they're attached. The solution is to accommodate pipe movement.

What You'll Need

- Screwdriver
- Lineman's pliers
- Suspension pipe clamps and screws
- Stainless steel screws

How You Do It

1. Trace hot-water supply and cold-water return lines from the boiler. They're usually secured to supports with U-shaped metal straps. Use a screwdriver and lineman's pliers to remove the straps.

2. Replace each strap with a slide-on suspension pipe clamp. Screw them to the wood with stainless steel screws.

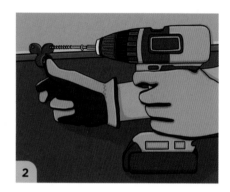

Quiet a Banging Steam-Heat Radiator

TIME: 15 minutes / **SKILL LEVEL:** Easy

This common condition is usually caused by condensation water that is supposed to run off back to the boiler but is instead bottled up because the radiator is not sitting level. This project is easier with a helper.

What You'll Need

- Level
- Pipe wrench
- Furniture coasters

How You Do It

1. Turn the heat off and let the radiator cool. Set a level on the radiator.

2. Use a pipe wrench to loosen the union nut holding the spud to valve. Check level front to back on the valve side and add coasters under the back or front legs to make it plumb (holding the level vertically to the radiator). Align the spud and tighten the union nut just enough to hold the radiator to the valve.

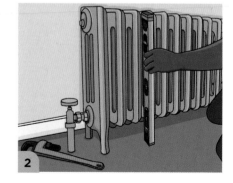

3. Lift the opposite end and add coasters under both legs. Check level side to side and front to back and add or remove coasters as necessary. Once the radiator is level both ways, tighten the union nut.

Seal and Insulate Heating Ducts

TIME: 1 hour (depending on number and length of ductwork) / **SKILL LEVEL:** Easy

Heated air in a forced-air system can leak out of ductwork, adding as much as 20 percent to your yearly energy bill. That makes sealing and insulating ducts a high return-on-investment project.

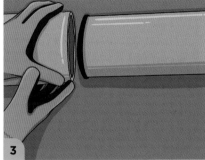

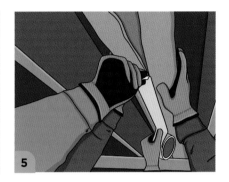

What You'll Need

- Eye protection
- Work gloves
- Duct mastic sealant
- 2" brush
- Foil HVAC tape
- Tape measure
- Utility knife
- Long metal straightedge
- Duct insulation or duct sleeve insulation
- Foil insulation tape

How You Do It

1. Turn off heating and air-conditioning. Inspect ductwork and determine the supply trunks (warm air to rooms) and returns (cool air back to furnace). Seal all ductwork but only insulate supply ducts.

2. Wear eye protection and work gloves. Brush on a thick layer of mastic to seal curved seams at elbows and bends (follow the manufacturer's directions). Securely tape straight-line seams with foil HVAC tape.

3. Wrap round supply ducts with pre-taped circular insulation sleeves (buy sleeves that match the ducts' diameter). For hard-to-reach runs, slip off the nearest elbow, position the supplied plastic slip cap on the duct end, and slide the sleeve into place.

4. For large or squared-off supply ducts, measure the circumference or perimeter of the duct. Unroll duct batt insulation and use a utility knife and a long metal straightedge to cut the batting to match.

5. Wrap the duct with insulation (easier with a helper). Tape the seam where the two edges of the insulation meet, using foil insulation tape. Insulate all supply lines.

White Flag

Underperforming older forced-air systems can benefit from a professional solution. The latest technology for sealing HVAC ductwork—especially inside walls or other impossible-to-reach areas—is internal sealant. The involves blowing aerosolized sealant liquid into ducts, under pressure. The rubbery sealant clings to leaks, drying rapidly, and sealing them from the inside. This is not a DIY technique. The HVAC pros that provide the service can use their equipment to determine exactly how much leakage is occurring.

● ● ○

Install a Programmable Thermostat

TIME: 45 minutes / **SKILL LEVEL:** Moderate

Digital technology has been around for decades, but there are still many analog mercury-switch home thermostats hanging around. These can be money wasters because they can't be set to go on or off based on need. A digital thermostat offers more control. This project describes installing a basic "set it once, and you're done" programmable thermostat, but the installation process is basically the same for any programmable unit.

Money Wise

Only pay for the digital thermostat you'll use. A basic model, like the one here, costs $40 to $50. It can adjust temperature at different times and days. Prices rise with the number of features. The most expensive are smart thermostats. Wi-Fi- or Bluetooth-enabled, these can be programmed and controlled from a smartphone, tablet, or computer. Features include "auto-away" functions that lower the temperature when the house is empty, energy consumption tracking, and more. Get the best bargain by honestly assessing how much information and tech you want to manage.

What You'll Need

- Programmable thermostat
- Screwdriver
- Circuit tester
- Painter's tape or masking tape
- Power drill and bits

How You Do It

1. Turn off power to the thermostat and turn off heating and air-conditioning. Remove the existing cover plate and unscrew the body. Remove and set aside. Use a circuit tester to check that the power is off. Disconnect each low voltage wire from the terminals. As you do, label each with tape marking the letter of the respective terminal.

2. Unscrew the mounting plate. Hold the cable containing the low-voltage wires so it doesn't fall back into the wall. Temporarily tape it to the wall.

3. Position the new mounting place over the existing hole and guide the wire cable through the plate's opening. Tape the cable to the wall again. Mark and drill starter holes for the mounting plate screws. Install anchors as necessary. Screw the mounting plate to the wall.

4. Double-check the manufacturer's instructions to determine the correct locations for the wires. Connect them to the appropriate terminals. Install batteries and snap or screw the thermostat to the mounting plate. Turn the power on and test the thermostat functions.

Safe at Home

Older analog thermostats—the round-dial versions—often have mercury switches. The mercury is hazardous waste. Do not discard the thermostat in household garbage. Contact your local sanitation department for safe disposal instructions.

Hang a Ceiling Fan

TIME: 90 minutes / **SKILL LEVEL:** Moderate

Ceiling fans help keep rooms cool or evenly warm. A ceiling fan can even alleviate the need for air-conditioning. They are available in styles ranging from Victorian to modern, and many feature built-in lighting and a remote. Look for a reverse-direction feature so you can reverse blade direction for summer and winter. (Pushing cool air down creates cooling wind chill; drawing cold air up forces warm air down.) The height of your ceiling will determine if you need a flush-mount or down-rod fan (angled mounts are also available).

How You Do It

1. Turn the power off to the room. Remove any bulbs and use a circuit tester to check that no current is flowing.

2. Remove the existing fixture's mounting canopy and unscrew the fixture from its mounting bracket. Unscrew the bracket from the ceiling box and undo the wire connections.

3. Use a flashlight to check if the ceiling electrical box is labeled "acceptable for fan." If not, remove the box and install a new fan-supporting electrical ceiling box (an "old work" box). Slide the new box brace up into the ceiling hole to bridge across the joists. Rotate the brace to tighten it in place. Slide the wiring into the box through a knockout and mount the box to the brace with the supplied hardware.

4. Fasten the fan mounting bracket to the ceiling box. Attach the down rod and canopy to the housing following the manufacturer's directions, running the wires through the rod first. Strip 1" off the ends of the wires.

5. Screw the fan mount to the bracket or set the ball mount in the bracket cradle. If the fan uses a remote, tuck the receiver into the bracket.

6. Connect the wires using wire nuts (ground—usually green or copper—to ground wire or ground nut in electrical box; neutral—usually white—to neutral; and live—usually black or red—to live). Follow the manufacturer's instructions and call an electrician if you're unsure the wiring is correct. Tuck the wires inside the box and secure the fan canopy over the box.

What You'll Need

- Ladder
- Circuit tester
- Screwdriver
- Flashlight (optional)
- Fan-approved ceiling electrical box and joist mounting bracket (optional)
- Fan
- Multipurpose electrician's tool
- Wire nuts

Ceiling Fan Size

The bottom of a ceiling fan should hang 8' to 9'—but at least 7'—from the floor. Blade spread depends on a room's square footage. For a fan with an odd number of blades, measure from the fixture's center to a blade tip and double that number. For an even number of blades, measure tip to tip of opposite blades. Blade tips should be at least 18" from the nearest wall.

BLADE SPREAD	ROOM SIZE
to 36"	to 72 square feet
to 48"	to 180 square feet
to 58"	to 350 square feet
60" and above	more than 400 square feet*

Rooms significantly larger than 400 square feet call for two smaller fans.

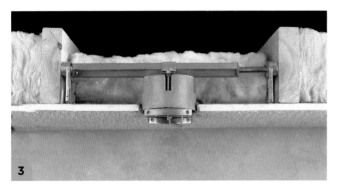

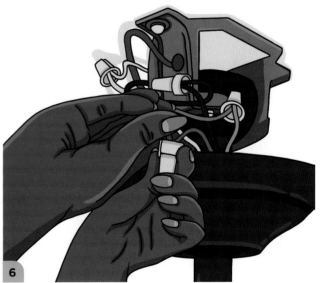

7. Install any separate light fixture, wiring it to the housing. Screw a light bulb into the fixture. Attach the blades if you haven't done so already (follow the manufacturer's directions—there are several ways to attach blades, but make sure they are securely fastened).

8. Add the pull chain if the fan has one and install batteries in a remote. Turn the power on and check that light, fan, and all features work as they should.

Balance a Wobbly Ceiling Fan

TIME: 15 minutes / **SKILL LEVEL:** Easy

A wobbly ceiling fan is nerve-racking and a safety risk. Wobbling can also shorten fan life. A balancing kit makes fixing a wobble easy and quick. However, consider replacing wobbling fans more than ten years old.

What You'll Need

- Rag
- All-purpose cleaner
- Screwdriver
- Tape measure
- Fan balancing kit

How You Do It

1. Dust the fan body and blades. Use an all-purpose cleaner to remove stubborn grime (sprayed on the rag rather than on the fan).

2. Unscrew and unfasten the ceiling canopy to access the ceiling box. Check that the box is approved for fan support and that joist mounts or bracket are tight and secure. Replace the canopy.

3. Check that the connections for the housing, blade irons, and blades are secure. Measure from ceiling down to each blade. The distance should be the same for all; replace warped, or damaged blades.

4. Clip the movable weight onto a blade. Turn the fan on and check whether the wobble is reduced. Repeat with each blade. When you find the problem blade, slide the weight in and out, turning on the fan each time to see which position ensures stable fan movement. Attach a self-adhesive fan weight at that location. Test one last time.

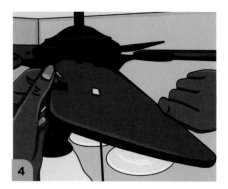

Clean a Dryer Vent

TIME: 20 minutes / **SKILL LEVEL:** Easy

Improperly maintained dryer vents cause thousands of fires each year. That alone should be reason enough to regularly clean yours, but proper venting also increases dryer life.

What You'll Need

- Screwdriver
- Small scrub brush with stiff bristles
- Shop vacuum
- Flexible vent ducting
- Duct tape

How You Do It

1. Unplug the dryer and turn off any gas supply. Pull the dryer out and unscrew the clamp holding the vent duct to the dryer outlet.

2. Use a brush to loosen debris inside the outlet. Suck out the debris with a shop vacuum. Repeat for the outside dryer vent. (You may need to remove the exterior vent hood.)

3. Check the duct for damage. If any, replace it. (Local codes may require replacing it with rigid metal exhaust pipe. Follow code requirements.) Tape the duct connections together with duct tape—or screw the clamps for flexible duct—at each end, to the dryer outlet and vent collar.

● ● ○

Install an Exterior Dryer Vent

TIME: 45 minutes / **SKILL LEVEL:** Moderate

Older homes often have basic wall holes for dryer vents or none at all. Open vents may allow rodents, insects, and cold air inside. Upgrading is easy and quick.

What You'll Need

- Tape measure
- Dryer vent
- Rigid metal elbow(s)
- Rigid metal duct
- 4 ¼" hole saw
- Power drill and bits
- Caulking gun
- Exterior caulk
- Foil duct tape

How You Do It

1. Unplug the dryer and turn off any gas supply. Measure from dryer outlet to the vent. Purchase the necessary vent, elbows, and rigid metal duct.

2. Use a hole saw (4 ¼" for a 4" duct collar) to cut a hole through the wall. Hire a professional to install in a masonry wall.

3. Slide the vent hood collar through the hole and square up the hood. Screw it to the siding with the supplied screws. Caulk around the edges.

4. Slip a metal elbow or rigid vent pipe onto the collar. Route the duct to the dryer outlet, sloping it slightly toward the dryer. Use foil duct tape to seal all connections and seams. Slide the dryer back into position, plug it in, and turn on any gas supply.

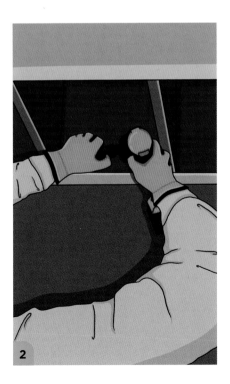

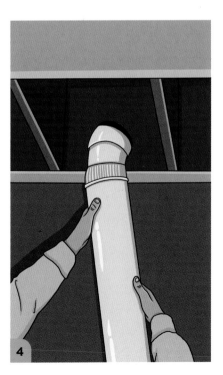

2. Structural Openings

A home's windows and doors are the most used, and abused, structural components. They are crucial, providing access to people and airflow and preventing water and pest infiltration. They are also essential to home security. Regardless, these openings have a way of blending into the background.

Windows

Most houses have more windows than doors. Door sizes are fairly standard, but window size and type varies quite a bit. Here are the basic types.

- **Double- and single-hung:** These are common to a range of architectural styles. The window has an upper and lower sash. Only the bottom moves in a single-hung window, while both move in a double-hung window. These windows are often painted shut and experience other age-related issues.

- **Casement:** A more contemporary style, casement windows are hinged along the vertical edge and open out. The most common problems are crank malfunctions and misalignment due to window frame expansion and contraction.

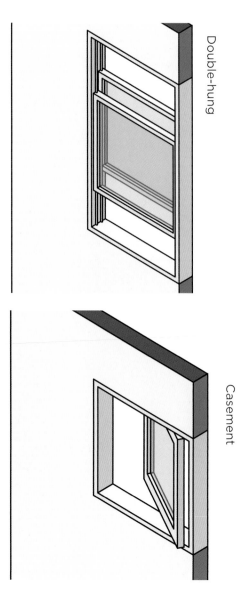

Double-hung

Casement

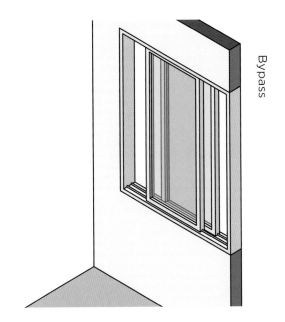

Bypass

Of course, interior and exterior doors aren't the only ones that see wear and tear in the house. Closet doors—bypass or folding—see just as much use. The same is true of kitchen cabinet doors. Sliding glass doors have their own malfunctions, as do less common "pocket" doors (sliding on a track into a wall cavity).

- **Bypass:** Also known as "sliding" windows, a movable pane slides in a track past a fixed pane. These often stick, preventing the window from freely opening and closing.

- **Transom:** Also called awning windows, these are seldom used anymore; they are hinged across the top and open out from the bottom. A similar type, hinged along the bottom, is called a "hopper window." These are common in older houses that were once heated by coal.

- **Fixed:** Fixed windows are just as they sound: They don't open. Plate glass "picture" windows are the most obvious, but these are used as decorative windows and in places that can't be easily reached. Breakage is the most common problem.

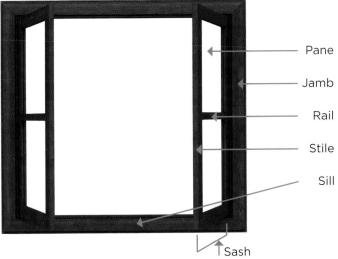

Pane

Jamb

Rail

Stile

Sill

Sash

Doors

Doors are simple structures, but there's a lot that goes wrong with them. That's a consequence of heavy use. Most problems are minor and easily fixed.

When buying parts or researching repairs, it helps to speak the language of doors. The first word is "handedness." This refers to the side the door opens on. Stand on the outside of any door (i.e., on your front steps for an exterior door and in a hallway for an interior door); the side with the hinges as you face the door is the "hand"—hinges on the right are a right-handed door. You need to know this when replacing a door or upgrading a lockset or a handle. For instance, if you've purchased a lever lockset to replace your current door handle, the lever has to point toward the hinges. Most locksets are marked with the handedness. In some rare cases, doors swing out. The handedness on an outswing door is reversed from above and is termed "right handed, reverse".

A lever door handle should always point in toward the hinges.

Install a Lockset

TIME: 30 minutes / **SKILL LEVEL:** Moderate

A new door lockset (the term for the handle with integral lock) can upgrade a home's look, and it can also bolster home security because older handles may not hold as strongly as a new unit might. Before shopping for a lockset, remove the existing unit, take measurements, and know the door's "hand" (see page 41).

How You Do It

1. Remove the existing lockset by unscrewing the handles on both sides. Remove the latch, latch plate, and door jamb strike plate.

2. Measure the backset—the distance from door edge to the middle of the handle hole. (The standard backset is 2 ³/₈" for interior doors and 2 ³/₄" for exterior doors.) Buy a lockset with a matching backset.

3. Screw the new strike plate to the jamb, over the mortise. Slide the latch assembly through the door-edge hole, making sure the beveled side is opposite the opening side of the door (otherwise, the door will not open or close properly). *Optional:* If the plate doesn't fit into the jamb mortise (the cut-out recess), outline the shape of the plate against the mortise and use a chisel and hammer to carefully remove additional material until the new plate fits.

4. Slide the outside handle into the latch body and then the inside handle (the one with the lock) into the outside handle and latch. Screw the handles together. Test the handles and lock.

What You'll Need

- Phillips screwdriver
- Tape measure
- Lockset
- Chisel (optional)
- Hammer (optional)

2

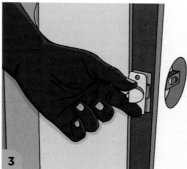

3

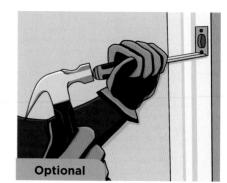

Optional

Pro Tip

A common problem with new locksets or deadbolts is misalignment; the latch doesn't slide cleanly into the hole. Locate where it is hitting the jamb to solve the problem. Open the door. Extend the deadbolt or door handle latch. Mark the outside edges with chalk, bluing, or grease pencil. Close the door and move the dead-

Install a Keyless Deadbolt

TIME: 45 minutes / **SKILL LEVEL:** Easy

Replacing an exterior door deadbolt with a keyless electronic unit makes it more secure and adds convenience. Never again misplace the key and lock yourself out. These units are usually battery powered and can be linked with home Wi-Fi and your smartphone. Most come with an alarm that triggers if the lock is forced. All are easy to install.

How You Do It

1. Unscrew the existing deadbolt and remove the outer and inner faceplates and deadbolt mechanism. Remove the existing strike plate.

2. Check the mounting plate against the door-edge mortise. If it doesn't fit into the mortise, chisel out material to accommodate the mounting plate.

3. Close the door and check that the deadbolt slides into the jamb mortise. If the deadbolt is misaligned, chisel out the mortise to fit.

4. Check the reinforcement plate (a separate piece that sits under the strike plate) fits in the jamb mortise. Chisel out the mortise as necessary. The strike plate should sit flush when installed.

5. Screw in the reinforcement plate with the longer, heavy-duty screws supplied. Screw the strike plate down over the reinforcement plate. Check that the deadbolt still engages properly.

6. Guide the control wire for the keypad into the deadbolt hole. Secure the keypad through the latch. Slip the interior mounting plate into position to hold the keypad in place. Screw the mounting plate to the keypad.

7. Screw the control unit to the mounting plate. Load new batteries into the control unit and fasten the cover over it. Program the keypad and connect to a Wi-Fi hub and/or your smartphone following the manufacturer's directions.

What You'll Need

- Phillips screwdriver
- Chisel (optional)
- Hammer (optional)
- Power drill and bits
- Keyless deadbolt

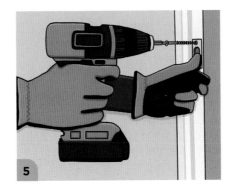

5

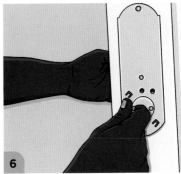

6

Fix a Sagging Door

TIME: 20 minutes / **SKILL LEVEL:** Easy

A sagging door usually sticks along the handle-side jamb when it is opened or closed. The problem afflicts heavier solid doors, rarely hollow-core doors. Exterior or interior doors can sag, and the problem is likelier in a busy house with many family members going in and out. Start with the simplest fix first and work up to more complex solutions if necessary.

What You'll Need

- Screwdrivers
- Hinge shims or stiff cardboard sheet
- Utility knife (optional)

How You Do It

1. Determine the extent of sagging by inspecting the gaps between door and frame along the top and down the latch side. The gaps will be noticeably wider at one end than the other. Start by tightening the hinge screws. Inspect the hinge-side door jamb for obvious damage such as splintering or cracking.

2. If that door still sags, loosen the bottom jamb hinge leaf. Slide two or three plastic hinge shims behind the leaf, and tighten the screws. Slide one less shim under the door-side leaf and tighten it down. Repeat with the middle hinge, using one less shim on each side than you used on the bottom hinge. *Optional:* Make your own hinge shims. Support the door along the bottom and remove the bottom hinge. Use one leaf as a template to cut shims out of stiff sheet cardboard, using a utility knife.

3. Check that the door opens and closes smoothly and that the gaps are uniform all the way around. Add or remove shims as needed.

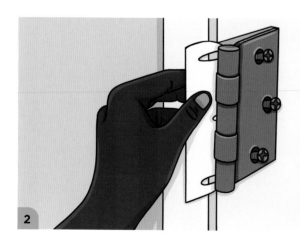

2

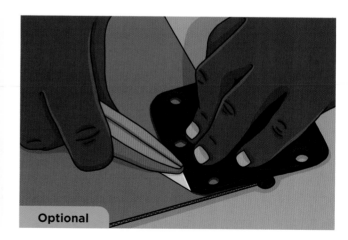

Optional

Fix a Sticking Door

TIME: 45 minutes / **SKILL LEVEL:** Moderate

Fixing a sticking door is simple, but you'll need one or two special tools.

What You'll Need

- Masking tape or painter's tape
- Carpenter's compass and pencil
- Power drill and bits
- Belt sander or plane
- Carpenter's square
- Paint or stain (optional)
- 1" brush (optional)

How You Do It

1. Line the latch-side door edge with masking tape or painter's tape. Open the compass to match the widest part of the gap. Run the leg of the compass down the door jamb to scribe the face of the door where it's rubbing.

2. Remove the hinge pins and place the door on edge, with latch edge facing up, supported by braces.

3. Use a plane or belt sander to remove wood along the scribed edge, down to the marked line. A plane is more efficient but harder for beginners to master. If you use a sander, work slowly and keep the sander moving. Regularly stop and check that the edge is square to the face, using a carpenter's square.

4. Rehang the door and check the fit. Plane or sand more wood as necessary. Seal the door edge with paint or stain to match the existing finish.

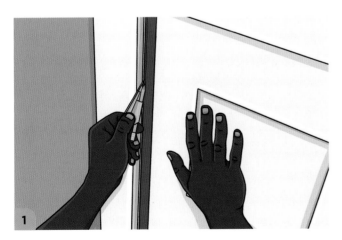

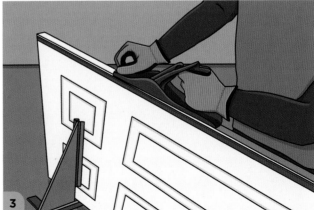

Hang a Prehung Exterior Door

TIME: 4 hours / **SKILL LEVEL:** Challenging

You can swap an exterior door with a plain "slab" door—a replacement that hangs in the same frame. However, this often involves chiseling, sanding, or other fine-tuning to fit the new door. A prehung door—a new door in its own frame—is easier. These come in many styles and materials. Prehung units include weather stripping and everything you need to secure it in the opening. Installation is straightforward and usually eliminates the need for chiseling.

What You'll Need

- Prehung exterior door
- Stepladder
- Pry bar
- Tape measure
- Notepad and pen
- Screwdriver
- Utility knife
- Hammer
- Reciprocating saw
- Level
- Carpenter's square
- Wood shims
- PVC cement
- Exterior adhesive caulk
- Caulk gun
- Power drill and bits
- Countersink bit
- New lockset (if not included with the prehung door)
- Handsaw (optional)
- Unfaced fiberglass insulation (optional)

How You Do It

1. Use a pry bar to remove existing interior trim. Measure the outside dimension height and width of the existing frame and door. Measure jamb depth. Write the measurements down. Unscrew and remove any storm or screen door.

2. Score the seam between the exterior trim and frame with a utility knife. Pry off the exterior trim. Tap out the existing door hinge pins from the bottom with a screwdriver and hammer. Remove the door.

3. Unscrew the strike plates for the latch and deadbolt. Cut around the frame with a reciprocating saw to sever fasteners. Push the old frame out of the doorway from inside.

4. Use a level to check that the opening sides are plumb and the threshold is level. Use a carpenter's square to determine if all four corners are square. Shim or build up wood members to achieve level, plumb, or square.

5. Dry fit the new sill pan pieces. Slip the end pieces in place and cement the center section on top of them with PVC cement. When the pieces are cured, remove the sill pan as one piece.

6. Line the sill with exterior adhesive caulk and seat the pan. Let it cure for the time recommended by the manufacturer. Caulk the sill seams along the back and between the sill pieces.

7. Remove the lockset plug in the prehung frame. Drill an access hole for any doorbell wires. Unwrap exterior protection from the prehung unit. Lay a bead of exterior sealant caulk along the inside of the brick mold (the lip around the prehung frame).

Pro Tip

This project is not technically demanding but takes time and effort. You need a helper; don't attempt installation without one.

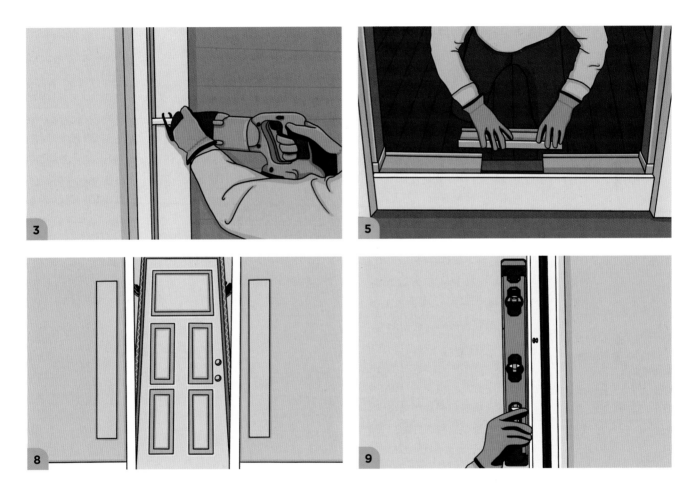

8. Set the door on the sill and then slowly ease the door and frame back into the wall. Pull any doorbell wires through the hole in the prehung frame.

9. Use a countersink drill bit to countersink pilot holes next to the hinges, top to bottom, and at the same places on the opposite side, and next to the strike plate. Drive the supplied screws halfway into the middle holes. Hold a level on the front and inside of the frame to check level and plumb. Drive the remaining screws halfway into the frame holes on the hinge side of the unit.

(continued) ▶

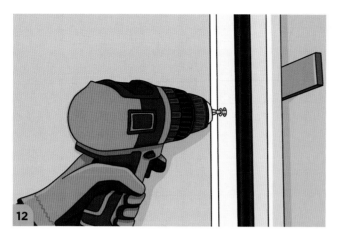

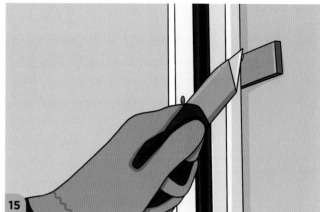

10. Check inside that the unit looks centered and use a level to check plumb on the inside hinge edge. Drive shims behind the screw locations on the hinge side and tighten the screws all the way down.

11. Close the door and measure where the weather stripping lines up on the door, top, middle, and bottom. The measurements should be the same, or you'll need to slightly force the frame outside where it is too far in. Drive the screws halfway in at the top and bottom and drive shims at the screw locations and behind the strike plate (as well as the deadbolt strike plate if there is one).

12. Check the inside of the frame for plumb and adjust the shims as necessary. Drive the screws all the way into the countersunk holes and through the shims. Shim behind the second screw on the strike plate and tighten down the strike plate.

13. Lay a piece of paper on the threshold and close the door. You should be able to pull the paper out, but feel resistance. If the paper won't come out or pulls out too easily, tighten or loosen the sill cap screws to lower or raise the cap.

14. Caulk the edges of the sill cap and fasten the self-stick weather stripping corners over the caulked seam. Install the lockset (see page 42) and deadbolt. Check that they work correctly.

15. Cut the shims off flush with the frame using a handsaw or utility knife. Jam insulation into any gaps between frame and wall. Replace the interior trim or cut and install new trim. Seal around the exterior trim with sealant caulk and paint the door if desired.

●●●

Hang a Prehung Interior Door

TIME: 2 hours / **SKILL LEVEL:** Challenging

A prehung interior door is an easy way to update the interior look. It's also the ideal way to add a door in a newly cut wall opening. These doors alleviate the need to cut mortises or adjust a door to an existing frame.

How You Do It

1. Remove the existing door and frame. Unwrap the prehung unit and slide it into the opening so that the frame is flush with wall all around. Starting with the top head jamb, check level and shim to secure the door frame in place. Check and ensure the sides are plumb, using the level and shimming as necessary. Check level and plumb one last time when you're done.

2. Drive finishing nails through the frame, shims, and into the studs and header. Stop before the nail is flush and set each nail with a nailset. Drive nails through the shims into the stud, anywhere the frame does not cover the wall framing.

3. Check that the door opens and closes properly. Install the trim on the side opposite where shims stick out. Trim the shims flush with a handsaw or utility knife. Install the trim on the second side. Paint the door and trim as necessary. Install the lockset or handle.

What You'll Need

- Prehung interior door
- Carpenter's level
- Wood shims
- Claw hammer
- Finishing nails
- Nailset
- Handsaw or utility knife
- Lockset

Install a Storm Door

TIME: 1 hour / **SKILL LEVEL:** Easy

What You'll Need

- Storm door
- Tape measure
- Marking pen
- Hacksaw
- Level
- Power drill and bits
- Screwdriver

Storm doors defend against higher energy bills. Adding one in front of an exterior door is like adding a layer of insulation. They are also a way to dress up any exterior-facing door.

How You Do It

1. Before buying a storm door, measure from the door sill to the inside top of the door frame on the left, right, and middle. Measure side to side at bottom, middle, and top. Use the shortest height and width measurements and buy a storm door to match.

2. Screw the drip cap to the trim right above the door, driving one or two screws with a drill or driver. Measure from the underside of the drip cap down to the top of the sill. Subtract ¼".

3. Mark the supplied hinge-side Z-bar to match the measurement. Cut it to length with a hacksaw. Avoid tearing out any integral weather stripping. Screw the Z-bar to the hinged side frame edge with a screwdriver, using the supplied hardware. Screw the door to the Z-bar.

4. Adjust the drip cap so that there is at least ¼" between it and the storm door top edge. Check the cap for level and tighten it down. Check that the door opens and closes properly.

5. Measure from the drip cap bottom to the top of the sill on the latch side. Cut and install the latch-side Z-bar as on the hinge side, leaving a ¼" gap between the bar top and the drip cap. Install the lockset.

6. Hold the door sweep in place and mark it for cutting, if necessary. Cut and screw it to the storm door bottom. Screw the hydraulic opener mounts into the predrilled holes on the storm door and to the jamb, checking for level. Tighten or loosen the set screw on the tube to ensure smooth opening and closing.

3

5

6

Replace Broken Storm Door (or Storm Window) Glass

TIME: 45 minutes / **SKILL LEVEL:** Moderate

Storm door and storm window glass usually isn't tempered—it breaks as easily as window glass. Breaks compromise the door or window's insulation properties, so replace the pane right away.

What You'll Need

- Puncture-proof work gloves
- Tape measure
- Screwdriver
- Rubber window gasket
- Utility knife

How You Do It

1. Slide the lock tabs and remove the panel to a clean, flat work surface. Wear puncture-proof work gloves to remove the vinyl or rubber gasket around the glass channel and any broken glass. Measure the frame side to side and top to bottom to determine the replacement glass size. If the pane is just cracked but still intact, jump to step 3.

2. Unscrew and remove the retaining rail (usually the top rail) for the panel. Be careful not to damage the corner retaining keys.

3. Buy new glass to match (take a sample to match thickness) and a replacement gasket. Starting at one end, press the gasket onto the glass edge. Continue all the way around, until the two ends meet—trim with a utility knife as necessary.

4. Slide the glass into the frame channel. Fasten the corner keys into the top rail. Slide the opposite key legs into the frame stiles. Guide the rail down onto the glass edge. Screw down the rail and reinstall in the storm door, or rehang a storm window.

Install Bifold Closet Doors

TIME: 45 minutes / **SKILL LEVEL:** Moderate

Bifold closet doors save space, making them great for smaller bedrooms or hallway closets. Installation is easy, but pay close attention to plumb and height adjustments so the doors open and close smoothly.

How You Do It

1. Remove existing doors and hardware. Measure the opening's interior dimensions. Buy door sets to fit those measurements. Fill old hardware holes with spackle, let dry, sand, and prep the existing woodwork. Paint as desired.

2. Mark the center of the jamb on each side with a pencil and use a level to trace plumb line down to the floor. Measure, mark, and cut the top track with the hacksaw fitted with a metal-cutting blade. Allow for a $\frac{1}{16}$" gap on each end for expansion and contraction. Screw the track to the bottom of the header, centering front to back and side to side. Point the pivot bracket toward the jamb on each end.

3. Center a bottom bracket and mark screw locations on the jamb and floor. Drill pilot holes and screw the bracket to the jamb and floor. Repeat on the opposite side.

4. Tap the pivot posts into the doors' top and bottom holes (if the doors have an irregular panel design, be careful to install the pivots on the correct ends). Install the center guide spring centered in the top track. Depress and guide the top pivots for one door set into the top track. Guide the bottom pivot into place and adjust for desired height.

5. Set the bottom pivot in the appropriate bracket slot so the outside door is flush with the jamb; loosen the top bracket adjustment screw and slide the bracket until the doors are plumb (check with a level).

6. Repeat the process with the second set of doors. Attach the aligners, if any, on the door backs according to the manufacturer's instructions. Install pulls or handles and check that the doors open and close correctly.

What You'll Need

- Bifold closet doors and hardware
- Screwdriver
- Tape measure
- Spackle
- Small putty knife
- Sandpaper
- Paint (optional)
- 2" paintbrush (optional)
- Hacksaw and metal-cutting blade
- Pencil
- Level
- Power drill and bits

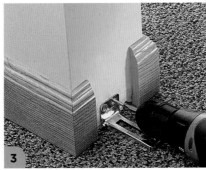

Install Bypass Closet Doors

TIME: 1 hour / **SKILL LEVEL:** Moderate

Bypass closet doors allow full access to the closet and don't require door-swing space. Less-expensive versions use only a top track. This project uses doors with top and bottom tracks. They provide more stability and less chance of damage to doors or hardware.

How You Do It

1. Remove existing closet doors and hardware. Measure the opening's interior dimensions. Buy bypass doors to fit. Fill old hardware holes with spackle, let dry, sand, and prep the existing woodwork. Paint as desired.

2. Measure the opening side to side at bottom and top. Cut the bottom wood support strip to length. Use a hacksaw with a metal-cutting blade to cut the tracks to length (an inexpensive miter box helps immensely in making straight, clean cuts) minus ⅛" for expansion and contraction. *Optional:* The steps here assume a wood floor. Follow the manufacturer's instructions if your floor is tile or carpet; some recommend cutting a track channel in carpet, and you'll need special screws for ceramic or stone tile.

What You'll Need

- Screwdriver
- Tape measure
- Bypass door set
- Spackle
- Small putty knife
- Sandpaper
- Paint (optional)
- 2" paintbrush (optional)
- Handsaw
- Hacksaw with metal-cutting blade
- Miter box (optional)
- Power drill and bits
- Level
- Wood shims (optional)
- Claw hammer

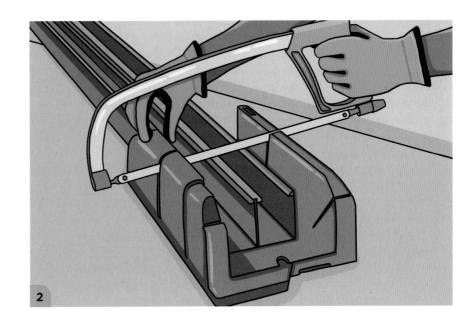

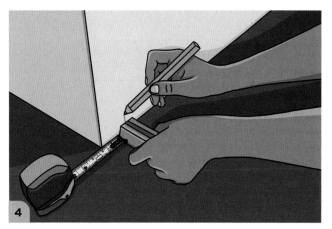

3. Determine top track orientation, if necessary (check manufacturer's instructions). Most manufacturers specify the track be flush with the front of the opening; center it front to back if you prefer. Mark the holes, drill 1/8" pilot holes, and screw the track loosely in place, leaving a 1/16" gap at each end.

4. Check that the track is level. Shim, if necessary, and screw it down. Measure according to the manufacturer's recommendations for the bottom track placement (usually requires an offset to match the top track), including any wood strip. Nail the strip in place and screw the track down to the wood.

5. Adjust the bottom rollers so that they are at the manufacturer's recommended distance below the frame (usually 3/4"). Attach top frame guides, if any.

6. Hold a door in front of the opening, facing you. Tilt the top toward the closet. Slip the top guide or slide into the rear track channel. Press up and set the wheels into the rear channel of the bottom track. Repeat with the second door and the front track channels.

7. Use a screwdriver to adjust the wheel alignment to eliminate any gaps between the jambs and the sides of the doors.

Pro Tip

Before beginning any project like this—requiring the purchasing of prefab structures and hardware—unbox what you've bought to ensure that all necessary hardware, fasteners, and special tools are included. If you don't check, you may find yourself making another trip to the store mid-project.

Install a Video Doorbell

TIME: 30 minutes / **SKILL LEVEL:** Moderate

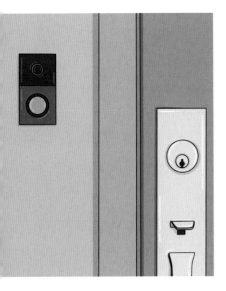

These days home delivery of just about everything is the norm. An unfortunate side effect has been "porch piracy"—thieves taking packages left outside a front door. A video doorbell can increase security and stop theft, and it is easy to install one. The doorbell camera feeds video to a smartphone or computer, recording anyone approaching the door. Just make sure the doorbell software is compatible with your computer setup.

How You Do It

1. Use the manufacturer's app to set up the doorbell on your home system. Shut off power at the breaker box. Remove the existing doorbell, testing that the power is off with a circuit tester before unscrewing the wires from the terminals.

2. Center the mounting bracket over the existing doorbell opening. Check the mounting plate for level, using a torpedo level (some manufacturers provide a miniature bubble level; if yours does, use that). Mark for the mounting screws.

3. Drill $\frac{1}{16}$" pilot holes. *Alternative:* To screw the doorbell to stucco or brick, use a masonry bit and anchors (usually supplied). Push the anchors into the holes.

4. Screw the mounting bracket to the wall with the supplied screws. Remove the manufacturer's miniature level, if any. Attach the doorbell wires to the mounting bracket terminal screws. Attach the supplied diode to the terminal screws if your chime is digital. (The diode must be positioned correctly for the chime to sound. If it doesn't, reverse the diode. You don't need the diode if you have a mechanical chime.)

5. Fasten the doorbell body onto the mounting plate, following to the manufacturer's directions. Tighten any safety screws meant to hold the body in place. Turn the power on and the doorbell light should illuminate. If not, remove the body and check the connections (reverse diode direction if the chime doesn't ring).

What You'll Need

- Video doorbell
- Phillips screwdriver
- Circuit tester
- Torpedo level (optional)
- Power drill and bits
- Masonry bit (optional)

2

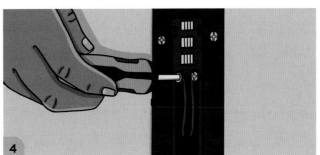

4

Tune Up Sliding Glass Doors

TIME: 20 minutes / **SKILL LEVEL:** Easy

Sliding glass doors are meant to be invisible but become all too apparent when they stick or won't open without effort. Head off any problems with regular maintenance.

What You'll Need

- Shop or home vacuum
- All-purpose, nonabrasive household cleanser
- Steel wool
- Screwdriver
- Aluminum lubricant spray

How You Do It

1. Vacuum the track with the doors closed and open. Clean the top and bottom tracks with nonabrasive all-purpose cleanser, with the doors closed and open.

2. Smooth rough spots on tracks by rubbing with steel wool. Lubricate the tracks with aluminum lubricant spray. Push the door back and forth to lubricate internal weather stripping. Spray the door latch mechanism.

3. Adjust the rollers to the appropriate height (usually about 1/4" below the frame), using the screw adjustment on the door edge. *Pro Tip:* The adjustment screw will be easier to turn if you lift the door off the track—or have a helper lift it—while you adjust the rollers.

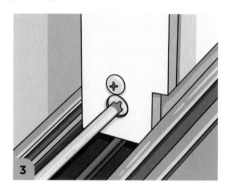

Replace Sliding Door Rollers

TIME: 2 hours / **SKILL LEVEL:** Moderate

Sometimes basic cleaning and maintenance won't revive sliding doors. If the door remains hard to open, the rollers may need replacing. Different manufacturers make slightly different designs, but all are similar. Roller assemblies are widely available at home centers and online. Remove the existing rollers before you shop to ensure a match. Because you'll remove the door, you may need to cover the opening with plastic if you can't complete the job in a day. You'll need a helper; this will be far more laborious alone.

What You'll Need

- Putty knife
- Screwdriver
- Sawhorses
- Door roller assemblies
- Polyurethane or rubber mallet

How You Do It

1. Remove any screen door by wedging a putty knife under the roller or spring holding the door to the track. Compress the roller or spring and lift the screen up and out. Set it aside.

2. If one door is stationary, use a putty knife to pry up the sill plate securing the door. Unscrew and remove any frame brackets. Slide the stationary door toward the center of the opening and lift it up and out.

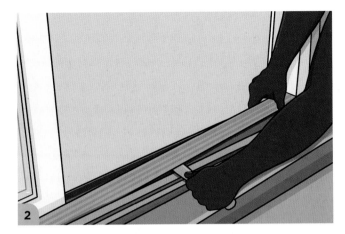

2

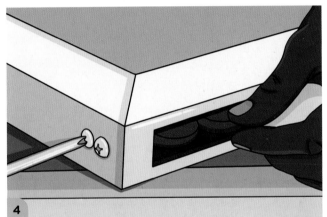

4

9

3. Use a screwdriver to adjust the door rollers up inside the second door. Lift the door up and out of the opening. Rest it facedown across two sawhorses.

4. Unscrew the screw above the adjusting screw on the door edge. Maneuver the roller assembly out. Remove the second roller in the same way. In older aluminum-frame doors, there may be a removable bottom panel rather than a roller-securing screw. Remove the panel to remove the roller.

5. Buy new rollers to match the old. Clean the door bottom with an all-purpose nonabrasive cleaner. Install the new roller assemblies.

6. Clean the door opening top to bottom, finishing with the bottom tracks. Check that the tracks are in good condition. If they aren't, slip replacement tracks over them.

7. Turn the adjustment screw to raise the new rollers up into the door. With a helper, lift the door into the opening and into the upper track. Guide it onto the bottom track. Readjust the rollers to the correct height.

8. Check that the door is plumb with the jamb and adjust one or the other roller until it is.

9. Reinstall the stationary door by tilting it into the top track and then guiding it into the bottom track. Screw on any frame brackets and tap the retaining plate in place with a mallet.

10. Install the screen door, if any, by depressing the rollers or spring guides with a putty knife and setting the screen into the top and bottom tracks.

Replace Window Glass

TIME: 30 minutes / **SKILL LEVEL:** Easy

Windows break. Double-insulated windows should be repaired by a pro, but you can easily replace a broken single-pane window. This method can also be used to re-putty single-pane windows in older homes, to conserve energy and lower utility bills. However, this process will only work for wood frames; find instructions for replacing broken glass in a metal frame on page 51.

What You'll Need

- Drop cloth
- Leather or puncture-proof work gloves
- Eye protection
- Putty knife
- Heat gun or hair dryer (optional)
- Linseed oil
- Replacement glass
- Glazing compound
- Glazier's points

How You Do It

1. If possible, remove the sash to a clean, level work surface. If this is not possible, make sure you have unblocked access to the window. Set down a drop cloth to stage supplies and catch any broken glass.

2. Chip out existing putty or glazing compound with a putty knife, but avoid damaging the frame. Use a heat gun or hair dryer to soften putty, if needed. If the putty is unpainted or the paint is cracked, you can brush on linseed oil and let it soften the putty. If the broken pane is intact, measure it both ways. Otherwise, measure the frame's inside dimensions, subtracting $1/8$" each way (for expansion and contraction).

3. Clean the frame channel of debris. Brush a little linseed oil onto the frame and let it dry. Press a bed of glazing compound into the channel.

4. Press the new pane into the putty. Use the putty knife blade to slide a glazier's point across the glass and into the frame. Use at least two points per side, or as many as it takes, spacing them 3" to 4" apart.

5. Roll a thin rope of glazing compound and press it along the edge of the new pane. Bevel it by pressing with the putty knife and then drag the knife along the bead at a 45° angle to the glass. Let the compound dry completely (may take up to a week) and then prime and paint.

Cure a Sticking Window

TIME: 15 minutes / **SKILL LEVEL:** Easy

This is one of the most common problems in any house more than fifteen years old. Wood window frames expand and contract, causing sticking. Homeowners also often paint windows incorrectly, gluing them shut with paint. The issue is easy to resolve.

What You'll Need

- Paint zipper or putty knife
- Scrap wood
- Hammer or mallet
- Silicone spray lubricant

How You Do It

1. Break a painted seal between sash and frame by sliding a paint zipper into and along the seam everywhere the sash contacts the frame. Paint zippers are available at hardware stores and home centers. A putty knife is a suitable alternative.

2. If the sash is frozen because of expansion and contraction, place a scrap piece of wood against the sash and lightly tap it with a mallet. Do not strike hard or the glass will break.

3. Once you've freed the sash, prevent future sticking by spraying the sash channel of single and double-hung windows with a silicone spray lubricant.

Tune Up a Casement Window Crank

TIME: 30 minutes / **SKILL LEVEL:** Easy

Casement windows are generally less prone to problems such as sticking. However, the crank can be a problem area.

How You Do It

What You'll Need

- Rags
- Penetrating cleaner
- White lithium grease
- Screwdriver
- Silicone spray lubricant

1. Open the window until the roller at the end of the extension arm is even with the track's access slot. Pull the arm down and out of the track. Clean the track with a toothbrush and rag, using a penetrating cleaner. Wipe dry and lubricate with white lithium grease.

2. Lubricate the track and hinges with silicone spray lubricant and dry with a rag. Reattach the extension arm.

3. If the problem persists, remove the extension arm from the track. Remove the cap covering the crank mechanism. Unhinge the pivot arms and unscrew the crank assembly. Remove it and spray with a solvent-based cleaner. If the mechanism is worn or damaged, replace the entire assembly. (Buy new cranks through the original manufacturer or at large home centers.)

4. Reattach the crank and lubricate the gears with white lithium grease. Connect the pivot arms and slide the extension arm into the frame slot. Check that the window opens and closes easily before replacing the cap.

Patch a Window Screen

TIME: 10 minutes / **SKILL LEVEL:** Easy

There are two types of window screen—aluminum and fiberglass. If you're replacing the entire screen, choose fiberglass because it's easier to work with.

What You'll Need

- Screen patch kit
- Heavy-duty scissors
- Hair dryer or heat gun

How You Do It

1. Buy a screen patch kit in a color and material to match the damaged screen. Cut it big enough to cover the hole or tear. Lay the patch in place adhesive side down and heat it with a hair dryer or heat gun on low (some are simple stick-on patches, but heat-activated patches are more permanent). Keep the heat source moving until the adhesive is activated and the patch is bonded.

Re-screen a Window Screen

TIME: 20 minutes / **SKILL LEVEL:** Easy

If your window screen has a large tear or hole, a screen is sagging or has a larger hole or tear, use this process.

What You'll Need

- Screwdriver
- Replacement screen
- Replacement spline
- Scissors or utility knife
- Spline tool

How You Do It

1. Use a screwdriver to pry up the spline and remove the screen. Buy new screening and replacement spline to match. Buy a screen roll size that will cover the screen with 2" extra on each side.

2. Unroll the new screen and center over the frame (the side with the channel). Cut the screen to size with scissors or a utility knife. Stretch it taut (this will be easier with a helper).

3. Starting at a corner, press the spline end into the channel. Use a spline tool to push the spline into the channel rolling steadily along its length. If the screen wrinkles, stop, pull out some of the spline, and begin again. When done, cut off excess screen around the edges.

3. Plumbing

Modern plumbing is a key difference between today's house construction and the structures built around the turn of the twentieth century. Even so, residential plumbing relies on basic physics. Household water comes in through a municipal water source or a well, runs through a water meter and main water valve, and is routed to branch lines throughout the house. Water to sinks, tubs, and showers goes to through a water heater. Depending on the type of heating, plumbing may also serve HVAC fixtures. Individual shutoff valves for each branch allow you to make repairs.

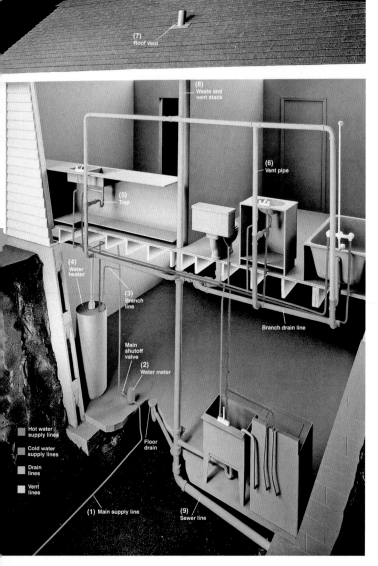

The flip side to water supply is the drain, waste, and vent (DWV) system. Water drained from sinks, tubs, and toilets is routed through branch waste lines to a main waste "stack," a large-diameter pipe that carries waste out to the sewer or a septic system. The vertical waste stack is vented through the roof to maintain positive pressure. Individual toilets are often vented as well. All toilets have a trap between the fixture and waste line, which stops waste and noxious gasses from backing up into the house. Maintaining drain pressure is why every drain—except in-ground drains—has a trap as well. Those traps are common spots for clogs.

Plumbing is so essential that repairs are often the first projects DIYers tackle. Upgrading plumbing fixtures can also offer big payback; bathroom and kitchen upgrades consistently rank high for improving home resale value.

Water Quality and Pressure

A good place to start building plumbing skills and knowledge is by testing water quality and pressure. These are less of a concern on municipal systems than for a well. In any case, water-quality tests and pressure testers are available at hardware stores and home centers. The best test kits supply a sample vial that is filled from several taps in the house and then sent to a lab. Water-pressure testers are attached to an outside water spigot. Turn the water on and read the tester (good residential pressure is 80 pounds per square inch).

Pipes and Valves

There are various types of plumbing pipes in a house. Different materials are used for different applications, exploiting the best qualities of each material. Fittings that mate to pipes may be threaded, slip-on, or compression. Code mandates specific pipes for certain applications, but in much home plumbing, it's acceptable to replace something like copper with another material, such as PEX. Here's a quick overview of the materials you're likely to find and work with.

- **PVC:** Some of the most common pipe, PVC comes in many diameters. It is durable, easy to work with, and safe for drinking water. The two basic types are Schedule 40, used for general plumbing, and thicker, stiffer Schedule 80, used for high-pressure lines. CPVC is formulated to carry extremely hot water. PVC pipes are classed by inside diameter; CPVC is measured by outside diameter.

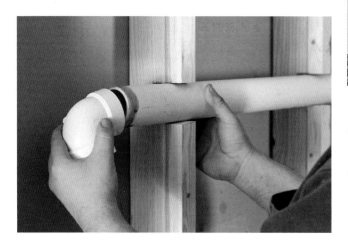

- **Cast iron:** Before PVC, cast iron was the most common plumbing pipe. Now, it's used mostly for vertical waste stacks. Repairs to existing cast iron plumbing are usually made with PVC pipe. Black iron pipes are used exclusively to carry natural gas.

- **Copper:** The two types of copper pipe are rigid, for cold water supply, and smaller diameter flexible tubes for fixture supply lines.

- **Braided metal:** These are used specifically to service individual fixtures such as faucets.

- **Stainless steel:** Both uncoated and coated stainless steel are used as supply lines for gas appliances.

- **PEX:** Cross-linked polyethylene (PEX) is the most recent development in pipe technology. This can be used throughout the house to run new lines or replace old. PEX is durable, easy to work with, and approved (even mandated) by most local codes.

- **Supply lines:** Some tubing is used just for supply to smaller fixtures like faucets or toilets. These come in preset lengths and are flexible to suit specific installations. They are easy to install.

- **Fixture shutoffs:** Installed right before individual fixtures, these allow you to quickly and easily shut off water supply to repair or replace the fixture.

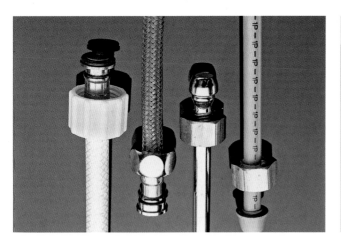

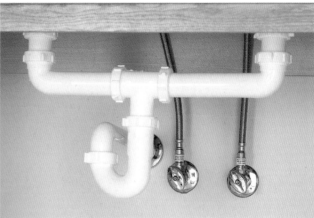

Water that flows through pipes must be controlled with valves. Several kinds give the homeowner control over the system and individual fixtures and prevent any leak from becoming catastrophic.

- **Supply shutoffs:** You'll often find these in basements or crawl spaces or right before large fixtures such as a water heater. Ball valves allow you to isolate water supply behind a stretch of pipe that needs repair.

- **Integral shutoffs:** Some fixtures, such as shower controls, have integral shutoffs. These make localized repairs less disruptive to the system (i.e., you can still use the toilet while repairing a shower).

SkillBuilder

TIME: 20 minutes / **SKILL LEVEL:** Easy

PVC pipe revolutionized residential plumbing. It is nearly indestructible and simple to fabricate. Learning PVC pipe and fitting basics takes only a few minutes. PVC pipes are marked with the diameter; buy fittings to match.

What You'll Need

- PVC pipe and fittings
- Tape measure
- Permanent marker, such as Sharpie
- Power miter saw or hacksaw and miter box
- Utility knife or PVC deburring tool
- PVC primer and cement

How You Do It

1. Measure, mark, and cut the pipe. Smaller diameters can be cut with a miter saw (also called a chop saw); larger diameters are better cut with a hacksaw and miter box. Use a utility knife or deburring tool to clean up cut edges.

2. Dry fit pipes and fittings together. "Key" pipes and fittings with marks that allow alignment in final installation so that they wind up in the proper orientation. Mark fittings and pipe ends and depth of pipe insertion so that you can properly prime and cement pipe ends.

3. Prime the inside of the fitting and pipe end. Slide the pipe into the fitting mouth and align the key marks. The cement should cure in about 30 seconds. *Pro Tip:* There are primer-and-cement combination products, but many professionals prefer the control of using them separately.

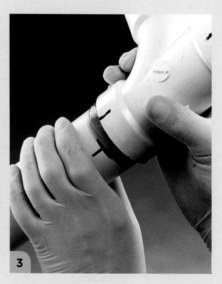

Install a Hands-Free Faucet

TIME: 1 hour / **SKILL LEVEL:** Moderate

Hands-free faucets have long been a staple in public restrooms but are becoming increasingly popular in homes. That's because they diminish disease spread and are easy for children and anyone with mobility issues to use. The faucets are available in most styles and finishes and for the kitchen and the bathroom. Regardless, all use the electrical charge of your body to complete a solenoid circuit, which turns water on or off. (It doesn't matter what part of the body touches.) The installation takes time but is not technically challenging. Installation is basically the same for hands-free, motion-sensing faucets.

What You'll Need

- **Hands-free faucet and hardware**
- **Adjustable wrenches**
- **Slip-joint pliers**
- **Flashlight**

How You Do It

1. Unbox the faucet and check that all parts are supplied. Clear out under the sink and remove any existing faucet (you may need a combination of slip-joint pliers and adjustable wrenches to do this). Clean the sink top and lay down a towel or rags under the work area. Turn off the under-sink supply line shutoff valves.

2. Guide the faucet's mounting post and supply hookups, along with the LED wire, through the escutcheon plate (you won't need this for a single-hole sink) and then through the central hole (shown detached for detail).

3. Slide the mounting bracket onto the post, being careful not to crimp the LED wire or supply lines. Check the manufacturer's instructions to ensure the bracket is positioned correctly, with the proper side facing down.

4. Hand tighten the mounting nut. Check that the faucet body is oriented correctly on top of the sink and that the LED light is facing forward. Tighten the mounting nut with an adjustable wrench or the wrench supplied.

5. Push the faucet outlet into the solenoid until it clicks and secure it with the metal clip provided. Tug on the solenoid to ensure it is secure.

6. Secure the feeder hose into the solenoid and secure it with the snap-on clip. Touch the cold-water supply or other ground and remove the cap from the LED wire. Click the prong into the matching hole in the solenoid.

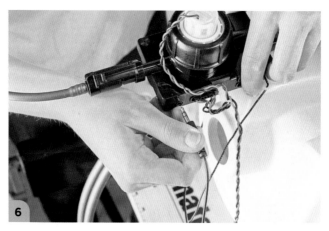

7. Slide the solenoid ground wire onto the mounting post. Tighten the second nut the same way you did the first. Insert batteries into the battery pack and attach it to a surface following the manufacturer's instructions. Insert the new ferrules and hand tighten the check valves. Connect hot and cold supply lines to the appropriate check valves (marked hot or cold). Hand-tighten, and tighten one rotation more with the wrench.

8. Close the faucet's handle and remove the aerator. Turn on the hot and cold water. Open the faucet and let run for one minute. Turn it off and replace the aerator. Check for any leaks under the sink.

9. Set the touch feature by turning the faucet on to the desired temperature. Firmly touch your hand to stop the flow. Tap to turn it on. Test different areas of the body. Motion-sensor faucets should work by moving the hand near the faucet.

Repair a Pop-up Drain Stopper

TIME: 30 minutes / **SKILL LEVEL:** Moderate

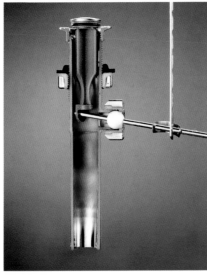

This particular how-to lies in a fuzzy gray area between repair and maintenance. Fixing a sink stopper isn't crucial to plumbing function, but it does solve an everyday annoyance and makes the bathroom sink more useful. The repair is a simple one to make but requires understanding how the pop-up stopper works (see cutaway at left).

What You'll Need

- Pop-up stopper replacement kit
- Bucket or pan
- Slip-joint pliers
- Pipe wrench
- Thread seal tape, such as Teflon tape
- Plumber's putty
- Putty knife or screwdriver

How You Do It

1. Clean out the under-sink area and clear off the sink top. Put a bucket or pan under the trap. If you're replacing the tailpiece, loosen the nuts on each side of the J-bend using a pipe wrench. Remove the J-bend and tailpiece retaining nut.

2. Disconnect the pivot rod from the drain by loosening the retaining nut on the side of the tailpiece with pliers. Compress the clevis spring clip and pull the rod out of the tailpiece.

3. Remove the pop-up stopper. Have a helper secure the drain flange from the top (jamming rubberized plier handles into the drain is one way, but just holding it may work) and unscrew the tailpiece nut holding the tailpiece to the flange. Remove the tailpiece and flange.

4. Clean the drain opening and underside of the drain. Thread the locknut onto the flange-end of the tailpiece, followed by the nylon washer and gasket, with the beveled side up. Wrap the tailpiece threads in seal tape. Roll a rope of plumber's putty and wrap it around the top drain opening and seat the flange into it.

5. Fasten the tailpiece to the flange from under the sink (with the rod hole facing the clevis), having the helper hold the flange in place. Tighten the locknut fully with pliers. Use a putty knife or screwdriver to carefully clean up any putty squeezed out.

6. Drop the new stopper into the drain with its hole or hook oriented to the tailpiece rod opening. Slide the rod into the opening and position the nylon washers on either side of the rotation ball, then tighten the rod nut onto the tailpiece.

You can purchase pop-up drain parts separately, but you'll save money with an all-in-one kit. These range from basic chrome-coated plastic pieces to high-end machined stainless steel parts, from $10 to more than $40. Some include the tailpiece replacement (the instructions to replace it are included below). Others just offer the drain pieces. However, as functional assemblies go, a sink pop-up stopper is basic. Beyond appearances, there's no reason to pay more than about $15 for a stopper replacement kit.

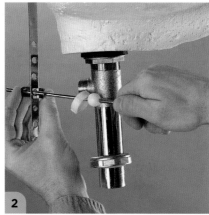

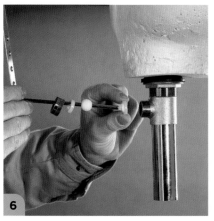

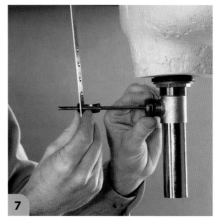

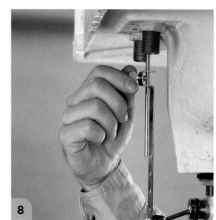

7. Put the other end of the rod through the spring front, clevis hole, and spring back. Compress the spring and slide the clevis in or out to ensure it is vertical.

8. Slightly loosen the clevis screw and pull the stopper rod up. Slip the clevis up the rod as far as it will go and then tighten the clevis screw. Close the stopper and fill the sink with water to ensure it seals the drain. Open the stopper and check for any leaks; tighten it more, if needed.

Pro Tip

"Staging" a repair is the practice of neatly laying out all the tools and parts you'll need. Getting in this habit makes any DIY project easier, quicker, and less frustrating. Arrange everything on a clean cloth, laid out as close to the worksite as possible.

Repair a Compression Faucet

TIME: 30 minutes / **SKILL LEVEL:** Easy

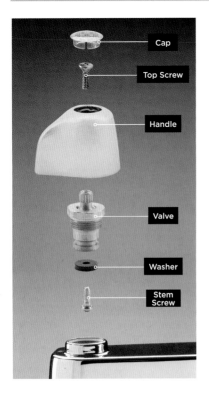

Compression faucets are common in older homes. The handle screw stem compresses a rubber washer when turned off, stopping water flow. When the washer is damaged, the water flow never entirely stops and the faucet leaks. You can buy a washer replacement (take the original to ensure a match) or purchase a complete rebuild kit—usually designated by brand.

How You Do It

1. Turn off the water supply. Open the handles to drain remaining water. Cover the drain with a rag. Use a thin-blade screwdriver or utility knife to pry the handle cap off. Unscrew the handle and remove it. Use an adjustable wrench to unfasten the stem and pull it out.

2. Unscrew the stem washer retainer screw and pry out the rubber washer. Use it to match the replacement. Screw on the replacement.

3. Replace any O-rings. Apply plumber's grease to each ring and rubber washer before reinstalling. Repeat the process with the second handle (rebuild both handles if you're doing one). Turn on the water and test the faucet. *Optional:* If faucet washers wear out too quickly, the stem seats may be worn. With the handle disassembled, use a seat wrench to unscrew the seat and replace it with a new seat.

What You'll Need

- Rag
- Standard screwdriver or utility knife
- Phillips screwdriver
- Compression faucet rebuild kit
- Adjustable wrench
- Plumber's grease
- Seat wrench (optional)

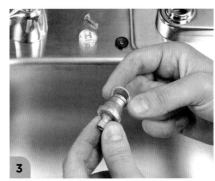

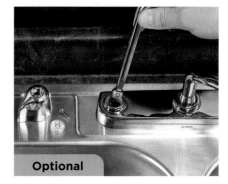

Optional

○●○○

Repair a Single-Handle Cartridge Faucet

TIME: 30 minutes / **SKILL LEVEL:** Easy

Single-handle cartridge faucets are popular not only for the streamlined look but because they're easier to operate with one hand than two-handle versions are. Most single-handle faucets use a cartridge system like the one in this project. However, cartridge construction and disassembly vary from manufacturer to manufacturer. This project provides a good baseline, but follow the manufacturer's instructions for your faucet.

How You Do It

1. Turn off the water supply and open the handle to drain remaining water. Cover the drain with a rag. Pry off the handle cap and unscrew the handle screw. (Some handles are attached with a setscrew; use an Allen wrench to unscrew.) Use slip-joint pliers or a crescent wrench to remove the pivot nut.

2. Detach the cartridge retainer nut with a standard screwdriver and pull out the cartridge with needle-nose pliers. Remove the spout and remove the existing O-rings on the body. Spread plumber's grease on the body before installing new O-rings.

3. Slide the spout back onto the body. Slip the new cartridge down into the body. Push a new retaining clip into the cartridge. Screw the pivot nut down and screw the handle to the top of the stem. Pop the cap back on and test the water.

What You'll Need

- Rag
- Phillips screwdriver
- Allen wrench (optional)
- Slip-joint pliers or crescent wrench
- Standard screwdriver
- Needle-nose pliers
- Cartridge and O-ring replacement kit
- Plumber's grease

1

2

Pro Tip

During cartridge removal, older units may break and leave a portion of the stem in the body. This is easily fixed with an inexpensive stem puller, available in home center plumbing aisles. The puller is plunged down into the fragment and then pulled out.

Repair a Washerless Two-Handle Faucet

TIME: 30 minutes / **SKILL LEVEL:** Easy

Newer washerless faucets have replaced older compression styles. Instead of a stem and washer, the faucet handles contain cartridges. The cartridges hold discs. The disc materials vary, but all are repaired in the same way.

What You'll Need

- Rags
- Allen wrench
- Phillips screwdriver
- Adjustable wrench
- Replacement cartridge
- Plumber's grease

How You Do It

1. Turn off the water supply. Cover the drain with a rag. Unscrew the handle setscrew with an Allen wrench and remove the handle. Unscrew and remove the stem screw. Remove the retaining nut using an adjustable wrench.

2. Note the cartridge's orientation. Remove it. Repeat with the second handle. Take the cartridges to the store to match new.

3. Clean the valve seat with a rag. Coat the seat and cartridge O-rings with plumber's grease. Secure the new cartridge in place, matching the original's orientation and with the tabs in the body slots.

4. Reinstall the retaining nut, stem screw, and handle. Run the faucet and check for leaks. Repeat with the second handle.

2

Repair a Ball Faucet

TIME: 30 minutes / **SKILL LEVEL:** Moderate

Ball faucets were the earliest type of washerless design and remain popular for their simple, single-handle look. A rotating ball covers or exposes openings in the valve, allowing water to flow from different supply lines depending on where you move the handle. Springs keep the openings closed, and worn springs or rubber seats are the most common cause of leaks. Repair one of these faucets with an inexpensive rebuild kit widely available at home centers.

What You'll Need

- Rags and a towel
- Allen wrench
- Standard screwdriver
- Slip-joint pliers
- Plumber's grease

How You Do It

1. Turn off the water supply. Open the faucet to empty remaining water. Cover the drain with a rag. Unscrew the handle setscrew with an Allen wrench. Remove the handle and unscrew the ball cap (this may require slip-joint pliers or a special tool, depending on faucet). Remove the spout body.

2. Lift out the cam washer and ball. Pop out the rubber valve seats and springs with a screwdriver. Wrap a towel around the faucet body and turn the water on for a few seconds to flush the valve seat. Dry everything.

3. Coat the O-rings with plumber's grease and slip them onto the body. Set the new springs in their holes. Push new rubber valve seats down into the holes (rounded lip facing up).

4. Install the ball, place the cam washer over it, and snug into place. Slip on the body and hand tighten the ball cap. Reattach the handle, tightening the setscrew just until secure. Turn on the water and run the faucet. Turn it off and check for leaks.

Install a Centerset Faucet

TIME: 30 minutes / **SKILL LEVEL:** Moderate

These are the most common and least expensive "lavatory faucet" (bathroom faucets). Centerset faucets have a central body on which two handles are mounted. Hot and cold water supplies are hooked up to their respective handles—traditionally hot on left, cold on right.

What You'll Need

- Rag
- Crescent wrench
- Basin wrench
- Putty knife
- Denatured alcohol
- Plumber's putty or silicone sealant (optional)
- Thread seal tape, such as Teflon tape

How You Do It

1. Turn off the water supplies. Open both faucet handles to drain remaining water. Cover the drain with a rag. Clear out under the sink. Disconnect the pop-up stopper clevis from the drain pull, under the sink.

2. Use a crescent wrench to loosen the supply connections at the handles. Use a basin wrench to remove the nuts holding the faucet to the sink. Lift off the faucet and clean the sink deck using a putty knife and wiping with denatured alcohol.

3. Follow manufacturer's recommendations to prepare the faucet base. Some recommend using the base gasket without sealant. Many people still lay a bead of silicone sealant between faucet and sink. Some pros discard the base gasket and pack the faucet's underside with plumber's putty. This is usually overkill. Regardless, don't use plumber's putty on cultured marble or composite surfaces; the putty can permanently stain those surfaces.

4. Set the faucet in place. Hand tighten the basin nuts and adjust the faucet position. Fully tighten the nuts with a basin wrench from underneath. Wrap the handle posts with seal tape and reconnect the water supply lines. Reconnect the drain pull to the clevis.

5. Remove the faucet's aerator and run the water for a minute. Check for leaks. Reinstall the aerator.

1

3

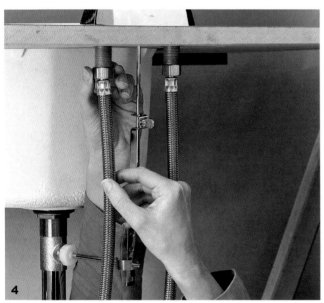

4

Money Wise

Centerset faucets are sold according to the space between handles, measured on center. The most common is 4", but measure your sink. Sizes vary, up to 12". Widespread faucets have a minimum spread but can adapt to a range of widths. Keep in mind that shiny faucet surfaces like chrome show soap scum and fingerprints more than matte surfaces do. However, it's visually pleasing to match other fixtures, such as the shower handles and towel bars.

Install a Widespread Faucet

TIME: 45 minutes / **SKILL LEVEL:** Moderate

Widespread faucets don't have a base, so they fit regardless of hole spacing. The look is sleeker than a centerset faucet and just as easy to install. This project will be easier with a helper.

How You Do It

1. Turn off the water supply. Clean out under the sink. Remove any existing faucet and clean the sink deck. Roll a thin rope of plumber's putty and place it around each sink deck hole. On cultured marble or composite sinks, use silicone sealant caulk instead, but follow manufacturer's recommendations.

2. Slip a handle tailpiece into the deck hole, orienting the handle correctly. Thread the retainer nut onto the tailpiece and hand tighten. Check that the handle remains in the proper position. Tighten the nut to secure the handle. Repeat with the opposite handle.

3. Screw the spout mounting nut onto the tailpiece and hand tighten. Check that the faucet is oriented correctly, then fully tighten the nut with a basin wrench from underneath.

4. Connect the supply lines from handles to spout by pushing each connection onto the valve and hand tightening the nut. Secure each connection by fully tightening the nut with a crescent wrench.

5. Wrap the hot-water supply line threads with seal tape and screw the connection to the left (as you face the sink) handle supply hookup. Tighten the connection with a crescent wrench. Repeat with the cold-water connection.

6. Attach the pop-up stopper clevis to the faucet drain rod (use a new clevis if one is supplied). Turn the water back on and remove the faucet aerator. Run the water for a minute, or until it runs clear. Turn it off and replace the aerator. Check all the connections for leaks. Tighten where necessary.

What You'll Need

- Widespread faucet
- Plumber's putty or silicone sealant caulk
- Phillips screwdriver
- Basin wrench
- Thread seal tape, such as Teflon tape
- Crescent wrench

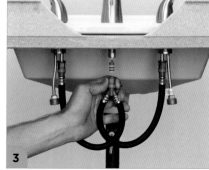

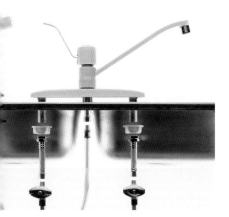

Replace a Leaking Sprayer Head

TIME: 30 minutes / **SKILL LEVEL:** Moderate

A kitchen sink sprayer is handy for washing dishes but wears out quicker than the faucet does. Rather than replace the entire assembly, you can purchase a replacement head online or at home centers.

What You'll Need

- Replacement sprayer head
- Slip-joint pliers (optional)
- Needle-nose pliers

How You Do It

1. Turn off the water supply. Open the faucet to drain remaining water. Unscrew the sprayer head base nut. (This is usually a ridged retaining nut between the sprayer hose and head and can be unscrewed by hand.) If it is stubborn, use slip-joint pliers.

2. Remove the washer on top of the spray head base. Use needle-nose pliers to spread the metal C-clip holding the base to the hose. Pull off the C-clip and remove the base.

3. Take the head with you to the store to match. You may need to disassemble the new head for installation. Slide the new base onto the spray hose and secure it with the new C-clip. Attach the head with the new mounting nut, hand tightening it. Turn on the water and check for leaks.

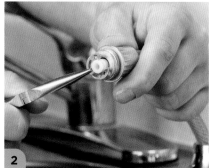
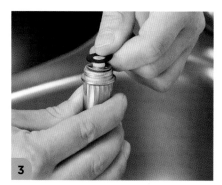

Install a Water Softener

TIME: 3 hours / **SKILL LEVEL:** Challenging

Hard water—water containing high concentrations of calcium, magnesium, and other minerals—is a problem in some parts of the country. Excess minerals lead to stubborn soap scum and hard, calcified buildup on showerheads and in faucet aerators. The minerals also cause white clothes to come out of the wash dingier than normal and can diminish soap and shampoo foaming. A water softener is the traditional solution. The system uses rock salt, which breaks down and binds with the minerals and is then captured by electrically charged resin beads. The minerals are flushed out a drain. The salt must be refilled every month. Most homeowners feel that is a small price to pay for improved water quality. Installing a water softener is a good project on which to practice plumbing skills. The installation here uses traditional copper plumbing, but you can use PVC or PEX. Just check that your local codes allow those materials. Although this is a good overview, different softeners may require different installation steps; follow the manufacturer's instructions.

Some municipalities require bypass valves and plumbing so that the water softener can effectively be cut out of the water supply flow. This ensures water supply even if the softener malfunctions.

What You'll Need

- Water softener
- Tape measure
- Tubing cutter
- Lead-free solder
- Propane torch
- Slip-joint pliers or crescent wrench
- Pipe wrench
- Steel wool
- Soldering paste (flux)
- Bonding clamp (optional)

How You Do It

1. Unbox the system and lay out ("stage") the components where they will be installed. The softener should be installed as close as possible to where the water main comes into the house and before the water heater. Shut off the main water supply valve.

2. Install the bypass port in the softener head by clipping the port into the inlet and outlet ports and tightening down the couplings. Attach the overflow tube on the side of the softener.

3. With the softener in place, measure the distance from the bypass port to the water supply line. Cut copper pipe to this length with a tubing cutter. Solder threaded fittings on one end of each pipe for connection to the softener's bypass valves (see page 92 for soldering instruction). Use two wrenches or pliers to tighten the pipes onto the bypass inlet and outlet ports. Don't overtighten.

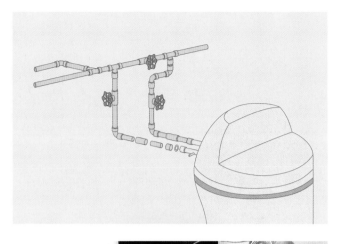

4. Cut the water supply pipe as necessary. Solder the elbow or other fittings on the opposite ends of the copper risers and solder the open side of each fitting to the supply pipe. (Be sure to thoroughly clean pipes and fittings with steel wool before soldering.)

5. Maintain electrical bonding by connecting the copper lines with a bonding clamp.

6. Clamp the discharge tube to the softener valve according to the manufacturer's instructions. Tie **the overflow hose and discharge tube together and route to a floor drain or utility sink.** The hoses should be secured in place at least 1 ½" above the drain.

7. Turn on the water main with the softener valve in bypass position. Open the valve and purge air according to the manufacturer's directions. Check for leaks and proper flow. Add salt to the tank (in this case, stacked on top of the resin bead unit in a single construction).

Install a Pedestal Sink

TIME: 90 minutes / **SKILL LEVEL:** Moderate

The pedestal sink has long been the fixture of choice for powder rooms and bathrooms where space is limited. They have a tiny footprint and come in a range of styles and colors. These are also less expensive than many other sinks and easy to install. There are subtle differences between the way different pedestal sinks are supported. Understand the mounting method before you purchase any new pedestal sink. Some are bolted to the wall, with the pedestal just covering the tailpiece and plumbing. The sink in this project requires firm wall support, including blocking between studs. Others are anchored to the wall but use the pedestal as a primary support. Regardless, proper support is essential to avoid sink breakage and injury.

What You'll Need

- Crescent wrench
- Socket wrench set (optional)
- Screwdrivers (optional)
- Pedestal sink
- Stud finder
- Drywall saw
- Drywall
- Drywall tape
- Drywall compound
- Sandpaper or sanding block
- 2×4 scrap
- Carpenter's level
- Grease pencil or carpenter's pencil
- Tape measure
- Power drill and bits
- Socket wrench set
- Caulk gun
- Silicone sealant

How You Do It

1. Turn off the water supplies. Remove any old sink and vanity, including the tailpiece and supply tubes, using a crescent wrench, socket wrench, and screwdrivers as necessary. Determine the location of the sink attachment holes and cut an opening in the drywall. Screw 2×4 blocking horizontally between two studs (not all sinks require this). Patch the drywall hole (see page 128 for the process).

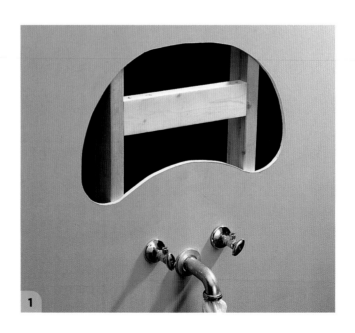

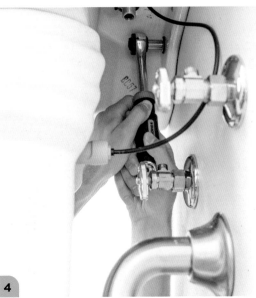

2. Place the sink and pedestal in position and brace them with scrap 2×4s. Check the sink for level and the pedestal for plumb. Mark the sink back position on the wall, including mounting holes. Mark the pedestal position on the floor, including any fastener hole.

3. Remove the sink and pedestal. Drill pilot holes for the mounting hardware. Place the pedestal back in line with the reference marks and use a socket wrench to secure the pedestal to the floor with a lag screw. (Some pedestals do not require this; follow the manufacturer's directions.)

4. Fasten the faucet to the sink. Set the sink in place against the wall on top of the pedestal. Align the mounting holes with the pilot holes. Drive lag screws through washers and into the wall, using a socket wrench.

5. Connect the pop-up stopper clevis to the rod. Hook up the water supply tubes and the drain P-trap. Caulk the seam between the sink and the wall with silicone sealant. Remove the faucet's aerator, turn on the water supply, and run the water for a minute or until it runs clear. Replace the aerator and check for leaks.

Unclog a Sink

TIME: 10 minutes (depending on severity of clog) / **SKILL LEVEL:** Easy

Almost every homeowner faces a clogged sink eventually. A lot of debris finds its way down the drain, and inevitably some of it sticks inside the drain pipe. A clog only gathers material and becomes worse over time. There are many simple solutions; use the one that works best for your situation.

What You'll Need

- C-clamp and shims
- Rag
- Plunger
- Bucket
- Slip-joint pliers or large crescent wrench
- Phillips screwdriver
- Flashlight
- Hand-cranked or drill-powered auger
- Wire brush or a probe

How You Do It

1. Start with the most basic strategy—plunging. For a kitchen sink with a dishwasher, stop the dishwasher line from releasing pressure as you plunge. Use a C-clamp and shims to crimp the dishwasher drain hose.

2. Fill the sink with a few inches of water. If there is a second bowl, stuff a wet rag into the drain, or plug it. Plunge the drain vigorously. *Optional:* For a bathroom sink, stick a wet rag into any overflow hole and remove the pop-up stopper. Plunge the drain until the clog either comes up or clears.

3. Where plunging doesn't clear the clog, place a bucket under the P-trap. Use slip-joint pliers or a large crescent wrench to loosen the slip nuts on the tailpiece and drain line. Unscrew the nuts completely and remove the trap.

4. Clear out the clog, using a wire brush or a probe. Reinstall the trap and tighten the slip nuts.

5. On a double-bowl sink, you may need to clear clogs beyond the trap. Put a bucket under the trap, loosen the slip nuts, and remove the trap. Clear the T fitting that connects the sink drains. Snake the drain line to the main waste vent.

6. Remove the wall trap arm. Use a flashlight to check inside the hole to see if there is any visible water. If so, clear the clog with a hand-cranked or drill-powered auger.

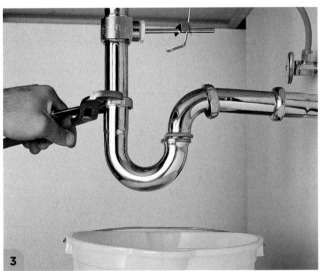

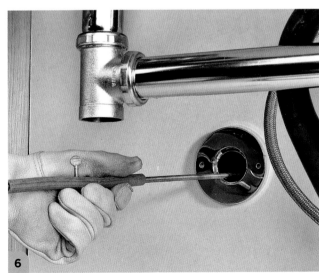

Adjust Shower Temperature and Tune Up the Showerhead

TIME: 20 minutes / **SKILL LEVEL:** Easy

The morning shower is an essential daily ritual for many people. Controlling temperature and flow make that ritual as enjoyable as possible. Modern shower controls are constructed with a simple device that stops the handle to limit the temperature. Some homeowners prefer hotter water. Changing the temperature limit is simple. It's also easy to clean or repair a showerhead to maintain the full force of the spray.

What You'll Need

- **Standard screwdriver or Allen wrench**
- **Phillips screwdriver**
- **Crescent wrench**
- **Painter's tape**
- **Thin wire**
- **Thread seal tape, such as Teflon tape**

How You Do It

1. Remove the shower handle. Knobs are unscrewed after popping the cap off; handle or lever controls are usually removed by unscrewing a setscrew on the handle using an Allen wrench.

2. Use a Phillips screwdriver to unscrew the handle control assembly. Pull out the limiter gasket—similar to the white plastic piece shown. This will have notches or teeth. Turn the gasket clockwise and push it in. Screw on the control assembly and check that the water is hot enough. Adjust if not. Replace the handle.

3. Remove the showerhead with a crescent wrench (line the jaws with painter's tape to avoid marring showerhead finish). Submerge it in a half-and-half solution of white vinegar and hot water, with a few drops of dish soap.

4. Clean the showerhead's outlet and inlet holes with thin wire. Flush the head with hot water. Replace a worn or damaged O-ring. Wrap the head arm threads with seal tape and hand tighten the showerhead.

○○○

Repair a Bathtub Pop-up Drain Plug

TIME: 20 minutes / **SKILL LEVEL:** Easy

Bathtub drain plugs are common DIY projects because they have a tendency to break. Simple in concept, the design is plagued by weak points. Fixing one allows you to fully enjoy a bath.

What You'll Need

- White vinegar
- Wire brush
- Phillips screwdriver
- Plumber's grease

How You Do It

1. Flip the lever to raise the stopper. Pull the stopper and rocker out of the drain. Clean the assembly, using white vinegar and a wire brush to remove any mineral deposits.

2. Unscrew the cover plate and pull the lever and linkage out of the hole. Clean the lever and the linkage as you did the stopper and rocker arm. Check for damaged or broken parts. Replace as necessary (replacements can be found at plumbing supply stores). Coat the parts with plumber's grease.

3. Reinstall the linkage and cover plate, and the rocker arm and stopper. Check if the stopper opens and closes completely. If not, remove the linkage and loosen the locknut on and adjuster and screw the lift rod in or out. Test the fit and adjust the lift rod until the stopper works correctly. Screw the cover plate in place.

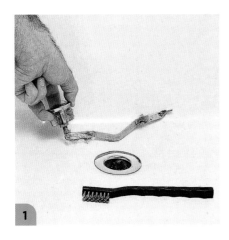

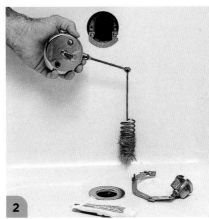

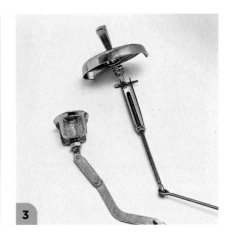

Install Sliding Tub Doors

TIME: 2 hours / **SKILL LEVEL:** Challenging

Shower curtains contain shower spray but are not an elegant option. A more upscale look, sliding tub doors are an achievable project for the home DIYer with a weekend to spare. The many tub door styles and finishes of tub doors provide the opportunity to add flair to a bathroom and even increase home resale value (kitchen and bathroom upgrades are historically some of the biggest return-on-investment projects when it comes time to sell).

What You'll Need

- Level
- Tape measure
- Hacksaw
- Miter box
- Masking tape
- Marker
- Power drill and bits
- Masonry bit (optional)
- Caulk gun
- Silicone sealant
- Phillips screwdriver

How You Do It

1. Remove the shower rod and curtain. Clean the tub surround and tub lip. Check the wall for plumb. Check the tub ledge for level.

2. Measure across the ledge to determine the distance between the two mounting walls. The correct door track length is normally about 1/4" less than this measurement. (Check the manufacturer's directions.) Use a hacksaw and miter box to cut the track to length. Center the track both ways on the tub ledge with the taller side to the front. Tape the track in place.

3. Position one door channel against a wall, with the higher side to the front. Slide it down over the horizontal track so that they overlap. Check the channel for plumb and mark mounting hole locations. Repeat on the opposite wall with the second track.

4. Drill pilot holes at the marked locations. (If mounting on ceramic tile, set the drill by using a center punch at the marks and then use a 1/4" masonry bit. Push in wall anchors for the screws.) If you're mounting on a fiberglass tub surround, use a 1/8" drill bit for the pilot holes.

5. Lay a bead of silicone sealant along the bottom of the tub ledge channel and dab sealant at each end of the ledge. Set the track in place. Screw the wall channels to the walls with the screws provided.

6. Measure the distance between the walls from the top of one channel to the top of the opposite channel. Subtract 1/4" or the distance specified in the instructions. Use the hacksaw and miter box to cut the header to length. Slide each end of the header into the top of the wall channels. Check that it is level.

7. Screw the rollers to the doors through the mounting holes. Tilt the inner door toward the shower. Set the rollers on the bottom inner track. Slide the door to the showerhead wall. If the bumpers don't touch the wall channel, remove the door and adjust the rollers.

8. Lift the outer door into position with the towel bar facing out. Slide the rollers into the track and push the door to the back of the shower. Check the bumpers and adjust the rollers as necessary.

9. Apply a bead of silicone sealant along the inside seam between the walls and channels, and at the corners where the channels meet the bottom track. Allow the sealant to cure before using the shower.

Regrout a Tiled Surface

TIME: 1 hour (depending on size of surface) / **SKILL LEVEL:** Easy

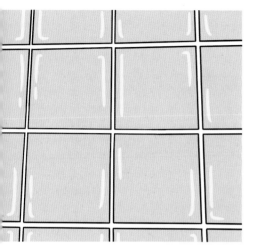

Tile grout serves a cosmetic and functional value. It can match tile color so that gaps visually disappear, or it can contrast to create a striking visual. More importantly, grout seals the surface from water infiltration that can cause rot, mold, and other problems. That's why it's important to remove and replace compromised caulk. Technically, this is simple, but it takes time and effort. You'll use a saw but can opt for a rotary tool equipped with the correct attachment.

What You'll Need

- Rags
- Plastic sheeting
- Painter's tape
- Dust mask
- Eye protection
- Grout saw or rotary tool and attachments
- Premixed, wet-use, anti-mold grout
- Grout spreader or float
- Putty knife or trowel
- Grout finisher
- Sponge

How You Do It

1. Clean the surface. Remove tub spout and handles and the shower-head escutcheon (if working in a bathroom). Line the floor with plastic sheeting and block off the room with a plastic sheet curtain. Cover any drain with a rag. Open a window and wear a dust mask and eye protection.

2. Starting at the top and doing vertical lines first, clean out grout lines with a grout saw or rotary tool. Remove the grout down to the base of the tile. Be careful not to chip tile.

3. Clean dust off the tile with a wet rag. Open the premixed grout and scoop a small amount onto the grout spreader or a putty knife. (For powdered grout, only mix what you'll use in 20 minutes.) Spread the grout across the tiles, forcing it into the joints. *Optional:* If you've grouted tile before or are grouting a large surface, use a grout float instead of a spreader.

4. After all the joints have been grouted, clean the tile with a moist sponge. Be careful not to pull grout out of the joints.

5. Allow the grout to harden for 30 minutes. Pull a grout finisher's ball end lightly down or across each joint. Let the grout harden for 8 hours. Polish the tile surface with a soft, clean cloth.

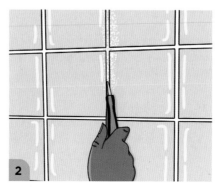

Recaulk a Bathtub

TIME: 30 minutes / **SKILL LEVEL:** Easy

Caulk wears out over time and should be replaced. This is especially important around the tub because bathroom seams are points for water infiltration. Never caulk over old caulk; the surface needs to be as clean as possible.

What You'll Need

- Drop cloth or plastic sheeting
- Utility knife or 3-in-1 caulk tool
- Rag
- Rubbing alcohol
- Painter's tape
- Silicone bath caulk
- Caulk gun

How You Do It

1. Line the tub with a drop cloth or plastic sheeting. Use a utility knife or a caulk removing tool to remove the old caulk. Scrape up any residue and wipe down all surfaces with a rag moistened with rubbing alcohol.

2. Carefully line both sides of the tub joint with painter's tape. The tape edges should be roughly ¼" from the wall on the tub's lip and about a ¼" up the wall from the tub.

3. Cut the end off the caulk tube with the caulk gun's built-in tip cutter (the hole in the handle's side) or a utility knife. Use a nail or the gun's wire to break the cartridge seal.

4. Lay any vertical beads first. Work from the top and move slowly and steadily, keeping the caulk gun level and bending at the knees.

5. Moisten your index finger and gently smooth the bead from top to bottom. Repeat the process with horizontal beads. As soon as you're finished, grab one end of the tape along the first bead, and steadily pull it away from the surface. Repeat with the rest of the tape. Let the caulk cure for at least 30 minutes and don't use the bath or shower for at least 24 hours.

Maintain a Water Heater

TIME: 45 minutes / **SKILL LEVEL:** Easy

A water heater is not only essential for everything from luxurious, long showers to washing your clothes and dishes; it is also an extremely pricey fixture to replace. Save money and a whole lot of frustration by taking simple steps to extend the life of the appliance and head off malfunctions and problems.

How You Do It

1. Shut off power to the water heater at the breaker box or shut off the gas supply to a gas heater. Close the water inlet shutoff valve.

2. Test the temperature-pressure relief (TPR) valve. (Some are plumbed into the tank side, while others are connected by a pipe.) Put a bucket under the drainpipe and open the valve momentarily, letting the tab flip closed. If water comes out after the valve is closed, it's compromised. Use a pipe wrench to remove it and buy a new one to match. Wrap the new valve's threads with seal tape and install it, tightening it with the pipe wrench.

3. Check the anode rod. Drain 2 gallons from the tank. Remove any cap over the anode rod, and cut out any insulation. Use a socket wrench with a 1 1/16" socket to unscrew the rod. Pull it out and check the thickness. If it's less than 1/2" thick, replace it. Wrap the replacement's threads with seal tape and install it. Tighten down the nut, cover with insulation if appropriate, and reinstall the cap, if any.

4. Drain water heater sediment once a year by attaching a hose to the drain valve bib at the bottom of the tank. Route the hose to a drain or bucket. Drain all the water. Close the bib, open the cold-water shutoff, fill the heater partway, and drain. Repeat until the water runs clear.

What You'll Need

- TPR valve
- Bucket
- Pipe wrench
- Thread seal tape, such as Teflon tape
- Anode rod (optional)
- Utility knife (optional)
- Socket wrench and 1 1/16" socket
- Garden hose

Repair a Leaking Shutoff Valve

TIME: 20 minutes / **SKILL LEVEL:** Easy

Shutoff valves are essential gatekeepers for home plumbing. They are simple and, for the most part, trouble free. But the gaskets that create a tight seal inside the valve can deteriorate and leak. You can cut the valve out of the water line and splice in a new one, but there is an easier way.

What You'll Need

- Bucket
- Crescent wrench
- PTFE valve packing, such as Teflon

How You Do It

1. Turn off the main water valve. Put a bucket under the leaking shutoff valve. Use a crescent wrench to unfasten the packing nut (the one closest to the handle), turning it counterclockwise.

2. Check the packing washer. Remove any pieces that remain and clean the packing nut threads.

3. Cut a short length of valve packing and push it into the nut from the pipe side, winding it around the threads. Tighten down the packing nut with the crescent wrench.

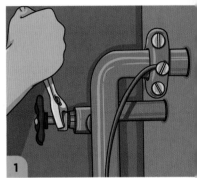

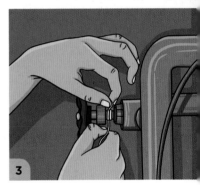

Patch a Leaking Pipe

TIME: 15 minutes / **SKILL LEVEL:** Easy

This is a simple fix for a surprise leak you don't have the time or opportunity to deal with immediately. Keep these supplies on hand to deal with an emergency leak.

What You'll Need

- Rags
- Rubbing alcohol
- Latex gloves
- Epoxy putty

How You Do It

1. Turn off the nearest water supply shutoff before the leaking area. Open faucets to drain remaining water. Clean the pipe and dry around the leak with a clean cloth.

2. Wipe the damaged pipe with a rag soaked with rubbing alcohol. Wearing latex gloves, pinch off a short piece of epoxy putty and knead it until the two colors blend completely.

3. Flatten the putty in a patch around the damaged area. The putty should be about ½" thick. Flatten out the edges to ensure the putty is sealing against the pipe all the way around. Wait for the putty to cure according to the manufacturer's recommendations and turn the water supply on.

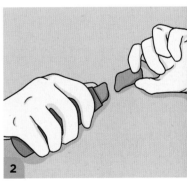

Replace a Section of Copper Pipe

TIME: 45 minutes / **SKILL LEVEL:** Challenging

Although you can replace damaged copper plumbing with PEX, many pros still prefer to swap copper for copper. The process is simple, but it takes a bit of finesse. The soldering skill you'll learn will come in handy for many household projects.

How You Do It

1. Turn off the water supply to the pipe. Mark end points for a section slightly larger than the damaged area. Slide the tubing cutter onto the pipe. Tighten until both rollers contact the pipe. Turn the cutter one rotation to score the cut line all the way around. Rotate in the opposite direction, tightening every two rotations until the pipe is cut through.

2. Dry fit couplings on the cut pipe ends. Measure from the coupling insets on both sides; this is the new pipe's length. Cut pipe to match. Rough up the outside of each cut end and the inside of each coupling, using emery cloth.

3. Brush a thin layer of flux on the cut pipe ends and inside the couplings. Slip a coupling onto the end of an existing pipe and rotate the coupling to spread the flux. Wipe away excess with a rag. Slide one end of the new pipe into the coupling and twist. Repeat on the opposite end.

4. Unspool about 8" of lead-free solder and bend the end to create a 2" angled section. Open the gas on the torch and spark the flame. Adjust for a blue flame 2" long.

5. Move the flame over a joint, heating the coupling and pipe on both sides. (If this is near wood or flammable material, use a protective sheet metal or fiber shield.) Heat all around.

6. Touch the tip of the solder to a seam between coupling and pipe. The solder should wick into the seam. Lay an even solder bead all around. Repeat on the opposite seam and the other end. Allow the joints to cool before turning the water supply on.

What You'll Need

- Tubing cutter or hacksaw
- Emery cloth
- Soldering paste (flux)
- Flux brush
- Rag
- Lead-free solder
- Propane torch
- Fiber shield or sheet metal (optional)

1

3

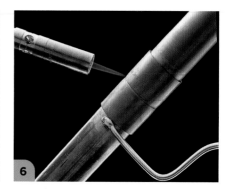

6

Fabricate with PEX Pipe

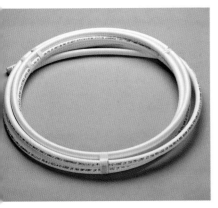

A coil of PEX pipe.

PEX (cross-linked polyethylene) pipe is a flexible alternative to copper, PVC, and other pipe materials. Used widely throughout Europe since the late 1960s, PEX has only been accepted and integrated into American plumbing systems for about two decades. Its popularity is driven by a combination of durability, flexibility, relatively low cost, and ease of fabrication. PEX can be run around corners and in other situations where rigid materials would require extensive fabrication. PEX can also be spliced onto almost any other type of pipe. Two types are used in the home: PEX-A and PEX-B. PEX-A is more expensive and better quality and is used with expansion fittings. PEX-B is used with handy crimp fittings. Neither should be exposed to excessive sunlight or chlorine, and they shouldn't be used together.

PEX is available in white, blue, and red; but the color doesn't affect price or application. It's sold in both spools and preset lengths and is available in diameters from ¼" to 1". Be aware that not all local codes allow PEX for every application. For instance, PEX cannot be directly connected to a water heater; there has be to at least 18" of metal connector tubes before it is used. Check local codes.

● ● ○

Attach a PEX Pinch Connection

TIME: 5 minutes (per pipe) / **SKILL LEVEL:** Moderate

Pinch connections are one "crimping" style to prepare PEX pipe ends for a connection. Modern stainless steel barb pinch clamps make connections easy even in cramped spaces.

What You'll Need

- PEX pipe
- Tape measure
- Marker
- Tubing cutter
- PEX quick-cinch clamp tool
- Stainless steel barb pinch clamps

How You Do It

1. Measure, mark, and cut the pipe using a tubing cutter.

(continued) ▶

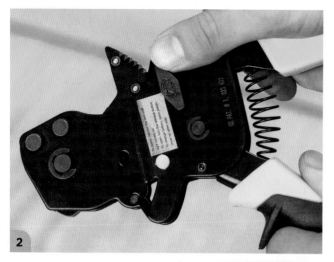

2. Check the ratcheting action on your clamp tool by unlocking it with the release button.

3. Slip a barb pinch clamp over one cut end. Grab the tab on the clamp with the jaws of the tool and tighten it just so the clamp won't slide but is not fully crimped.

4. Insert the fitting into the pipe end. Adjust the clamp to be perfectly parallel to the cut end, with a ⅛" gap between the pipe end and the clamp front edge. Pinch the clamp tab several times to tighten it until the fitting is secure. Release the tool.

5. Correct mistakes by slipping the clamp tab into a pinch clamp removal tool. Twist the tool back and forth until the clamp snaps and can be removed.

Replace Flapper Valve and Reset Tank Water Level

TIME: 15 minutes / **SKILL LEVEL:** Easy

When solving DIY problems—in plumbing or other areas—it's wisest to start with the most obvious and simple fix. A toilet that constantly runs, starts running for no reason, or takes too long for the tank to fill can be a basic issue. Start with the flapper valve and the water level in the tank. (Some modern toilets don't have a plunger valve instead of a flapper valve. These require wholesale entire assembly replacement when they fail.)

What You'll Need

- Sponge
- Flapper valve
- Phillips screwdriver
- Needle-nose pliers

How You Do It

1. Turn off the toilet water supply. Flush to remove all tank water. Sponge out remaining water. Unhook the chain from the flapper. Unfasten the flapper's ears from the flush valve body, and remove the flapper.

2. Clean the flapper seat. Take the old flapper with you and purchase a flapper that matches. Hook the new flapper's ears onto the flush valve hooks and connect the chain.

3. Turn the water on and let the tank fill. Flush the toilet. Check that the flapper is sealing properly. Adjust the chain length as necessary to ensure proper flapper operation.

4. A running toilet indicates the "critical level" for the float or cup is misadjusted. Adjust the water level for a ball float by bending the bar down bit by bit. Check after each modification to see if the problem is fixed.

5. Float cups have largely replaced float balls. Lower the water level by compressing the spring clip on the cup's side, using needle-nose pliers. Move the clip and cup up the rod a bit at a time, until the problem is resolved.

6. Some fill valves are controlled by a diaphragm. Turn the adjustment screw on top clockwise to lower the water level and counterclockwise to raise it.

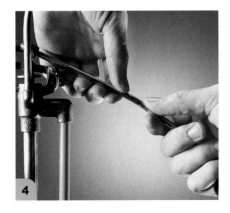

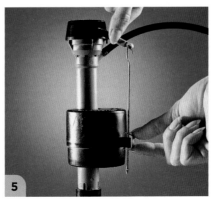

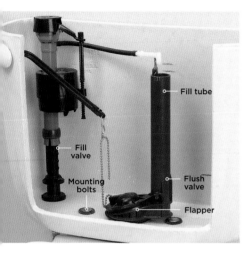

Fill tube

Fill valve

Mounting bolts

Flush valve

Flapper

Replace a Toilet Fill Valve

TIME: 45 minutes / **SKILL LEVEL:** Moderate

Your toilet flushes thanks to two valves: a flush valve and a fill valve. Replacing a fill valve is the easier project. A defective fill valve has obvious symptoms. If the flush is weak, the tank takes an inordinate amount of time to fill, or it runs constantly, you most likely need a new fill valve.

What You'll Need

- **Sponge**
- **Small bucket or pan**
- **Slip-joint pliers**
- **Fill valve kit**
- **Needle-nose pliers**

How You Do It

1. Shut off the water supply. Flush to empty the tank and sponge out remaining water. Put a small bucket or pan under the supply tube and disconnect it from the tank.

2. Loosen and remove the fill valve mounting nut on the underside of the tank. (Use slip-joint pliers to secure the valve inside the tank and stop it from spinning.) If you're removing an old ball cock valve, remove the float at the same time.

3. Slip the washer on the fill valve shank and slide the shank down into the tank hole. Check that the critical level (marked as "CL" on the valve) mark is at least 1" above the overflow tube. If not, adjust the level of the valve according to the manufacturer's instructions (usually involves holding the base and turning the valve post).

4. Push down on the fill valve's shank to seat it properly and hand tighten the locknut. Use slip-joint pliers to turn a quarter turn more. Hook up the water supply tube and tighten it the same way.

5. Remove any cap on the overflow pipe. Attach the refill tube to the fill valve and secure the opposite end right above—not inside of—the overflow tube (there is usually a bracket for this). Cut off any excess.

6. Turn on the water supply. Adjust the water level by compressing the spring clip on the float cup with needle-nose pliers and moving it up or down. (Some models have different control mechanisms; follow the manufacturer's instructions.) Flush and check for leaks. Tighten fittings where necessary.

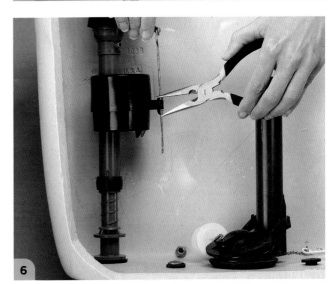

Replace a Flush Valve

TIME: 1 hour / **SKILL LEVEL:** Moderate

A toilet's flush valve is just what it sounds like: a valve controlling the amount and force of water going into the bowl. Malfunctioning flush valves can cause the flush to last too long or go too short, can leak in the connection between tank and bowl, or just simply may not flush at all. The replacement process isn't technically challenging. Leave enough time for the entire project so that the toilet is out of commission as briefly as possible.

What You'll Need

- Sponge
- Slip-joint pliers
- Large standard screwdriver
- Penetrating lubricant spray
- Hacksaw (optional)
- Spud wrench
- Flush valve kit
- Crescent or box wrench
- Level

How You Do It

1. Turn off the water supply. Flush to empty the tank and sponge out remaining water. Unfasten the water line connection from the tank, using slip-joint pliers.

2. Unscrew the bolts holding tank to bowl, from underneath. Use slip-joint pliers and a large standard screwdriver to stop bolts from turning. If the bolts are rusty, spray top and bottom with penetrating oil. As a last resort, cut the bolts with a hacksaw, sliding it in the seam between tank and bowl.

3. Unhook the handle arm and lift the tank off the bowl. Set it upside down on a clean, level surface with a towel underneath. Pull off the spud washer and use a spud wrench to unfasten the spud from the base (inexpensive plastic spud wrenches are available from home centers). Flip the tank and remove the existing flush valve.

4. Slide the new flush valve into the tank and measure to see if the top of the overflow tube is at least 1" below the fill valve's critical level mark. If the overflow tube is too long, trim it with a hacksaw.

5. Fasten the flush valve in place with the spud nut, by tightening it a quarter turn past hand-tight using the spud wrench. Replace the spud washer with a new one and install with the narrower side out so it sits correctly in the toilet bowl hole.

6. Gently lay the tank on its back and secure the mounting bolts by sliding each on through a rubber washer and then tightening the nuts on the other side over a brass washer. Tighten them a quarter turn past hand-tight with a crescent or box wrench.

7. Carefully set the tank in place on the bowl, seating the spud washer in the bowl hole, with the bolts down through the mounting holes (this will be much easier with a helper). Fasten the tank to the bowl by securing a bolt over brass and rubber washers using slip-joint pliers. Check the tank for level before completely tightening the tank down in place (being careful not to crack the bowl or tank).

8. Install the flapper and connect the chain clip to the lever arm. Adjust the chain to have a little slack when the flapper is closed (leave a small tail of chain for future adjustments). Attach the refill tube to the overflow pipe and turn on the water. Flush and check for leaks.

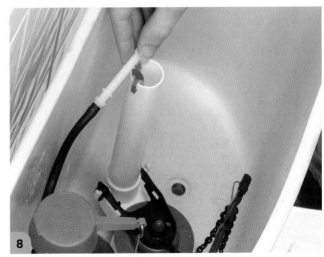

Replace a Wax Ring

TIME: 90 minutes / **SKILL LEVEL:** Challenging

Toilets are miracles of modern plumbing, but toilet leaks can be the stuff of homeowners' nightmares. This project deals with a not-rare but not-common problem of a compromised wax ring. The wax ring lines the opening that carries waste out and to the main vertical waste stack. However, this same process is used to replace a failed toilet flange (the PVC piece directly under the wax ring; when damaged, it causes toilet rocking and leakage). Use these steps for replacing a toilet.

What You'll Need

- Sponge
- Slip-joint pliers
- Crescent wrench or box wrench (optional)
- Large standard screwdriver
- Penetrating oil (optional)
- Hacksaw (optional)
- Socket wrench and sockets
- Putty knife
- Rag
- Mineral spirits
- Replacement wax ring

How You Do It

1. Clean the toilet in and out. Turn off the water supply and flush the toilet to empty the tank. Sponge out remaining water.

2. Use slip-joint pliers to unscrew the water supply connection at the tank. Hold one of the nuts securing tank to toilet, using a crescent wrench, box wrench, or pliers (whichever works best for your toilet). Loosen the bolt from inside the tank (usually a slotted screwhead), using a large standard screwdriver. Use penetrating oil on stubborn bolts and nuts. As a last resort, use a hacksaw to cut the bolt along the seam between tank and toilet. Repeat with the second bolt. Remove the tank.

3. Remove the cap over the toilet floor bolts. Use a socket wrench to remove the retaining nut (soak a stubborn nut with penetrating oil). Repeat with the opposite side and pull the toilet off the bolts.

4. Use a putty knife to remove the old wax ring. Scrape the wax right into a plastic bag. When you've removed as much as you can with the putty knife, clean remaining residue with a rag soaked in mineral spirits. Once the flange is completely clean, stuff a rag in the hole to prevent sewer gas from entering the room.

5. Inspect the existing closet flange for cracks, wear, or defects. Install new flange bolts.

2

4

5

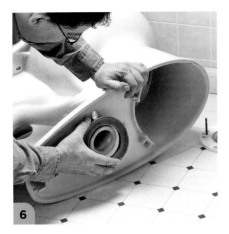

6. Remove the top protective covering on the new wax ring. Carefully slip the ring wax-side up onto the toilet horn. Remove the bottom protective covering. *Optional:* If your toilet is older, you may have a different type of 4" closet flange than what is shown here. For older flanges and toilets, install the wax ring right on the closet flange, not on the toilet. Regardless, avoid touching the wax ring.

7. Carefully lower the toilet bowl onto the closet flange with the aid of a helper. Slip washers over the bolts and secure with nuts, hand tightened. Tighten completely with a socket wrench, alternating sides, and being careful not to overtighten.

8. If the tank does not have a flush valve installed, install it now following the manufacturer's directions. Secure a spud washer on the spud nut.

9. Lay the tank on its back and push a bolt through a rubber washer and then down through one of the mounting holes. Thread a washer and an intermediate nut onto the bolt and tighten a quarter turn past hand-tight. Use the screwdriver to hold the bolt in place as you tighten the nut with a wrench. Repeat with the second bolt.

10. Place the tank on the bowl with the spud washer sitting flush in the opening and the bolts protruding through the mounting holes. Thread washers and nuts onto each bolt and hand tighten. Use a wrench to snug each bolt down but do not overtighten.

11. Connect the water supply. Turn the water on and let the tank fill. Flush and check for leaks. Fasten the toilet seat to the bowl.

4. Electrical Issues

Many new homeowners are fearful of dealing with anything electrical. That's understandable given the potential danger. However, the electrical service basics are fairly easy to master. Even if you never tackle an electrical project, it's wise to have an understanding of the system. That will help you determine if a problem needs immediate attention and understand what an electrician needs to do before you hire one.

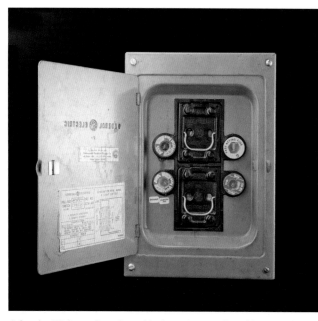

A basic 60-amp fuse box. No longer permitted by current electrical codes (modern minimum household service is 100 amps), this type of circuit breaker box is still common in older homes. Any fuse that blows must be replaced with one rated for the same amps.

The System

Electricity comes into a house through an underground or overhead main, runs through the meter into a breaker or fuse box, and is routed along different circuits to outlets and fixtures throughout the house. Each circuit services a given area. Circuits are uniformly 120 or 240 volts. Each also provides a limited number of amps.

Electricity is carried along wires protected inside cables. Circuit wiring includes a ground, hot or live wires that carry the actual voltage, and a neutral wire that completes the circuit allowing electricity to flow. When a circuit is overloaded—fixtures drawing more power than the circuit supplies—fixtures can be damaged, and overheating can cause fires. To prevent damage, breakers trip or fuses blow.

Those are the basics, but not all house wiring is created equal because not all houses were constructed at the same time. Depending on when your house was built, it may have unusual wiring and electrical features. That's because electrical codes, standards, and practices are updated as new technology and materials are invented.

SkillBuilder

Wire nuts, also called "twist-on connectors," are simple but can seem complicated. They safely secure stripped ends of two or more wires together. Wire nuts ensure wires stay connected and protect exposed, unsheathed ends from shorts or other mishaps. They are cone-shaped and colored by size. The sizes reflect the gauge and number of wires with which the individual connector is meant to be used. Although there are many different types, ranging from the general use to more particular ceramic versions for high-temp situations, homeowners will usually select from just five common wire nut colors: gray, blue, orange, yellow, and red. In reality, you'll use yellow or red in 90 percent of home electrical work. If you buy a bulk package of wire nuts, the package will usually be labeled with a chart listing the size of connector to use with given wire gauges and numbers. Here is a version.

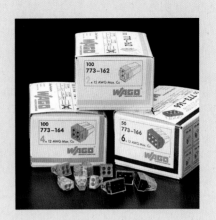

An easier but more expensive alternative are push-in connectors. These have holes for two to four wires. Each stripped wire end is pushed into a hole, where it is held securely by an internal clip. The connectors are offered for different gauges. They don't work in every situation—such as cramped quarters where wires have to be crammed in or in joining different gauges of wires—but they are an easy solution for many situations.

Wire Color and Size

Electrical wire colors usually (but not always) indicate what role the wire plays in the circuit. The colors represent the following: green or copper—ground; white or gray—neutral; black or red—live.

Wiring is also categorized by diameter, known as "gauge" and denoted by a hashtag. Gauge determines how much current the wire can carry. The lower the gauge, the bigger the wire diameter and the more voltage it can safely transport. The most common wire sizes in houses are #14 and #12.

Wire Size and Uses

GAUGE	CAPACITY	USE
#18–22	Low voltage	Thermostat, doorbell
#16	Light duty	Extension cord
#14	15 amps, 120 volts	Light fixtures, electrical receptacles
#12	20 amps, 120 volts	Large light fixtures, fans, GFCI, microwaves
#10	30 amps, 240 volts	Window air conditioner, clothes dryer
#8	40 amps, 240 volts	Central air conditioner, electric range
#6	55 amps, 240 volts	High-capacity central air conditioner, furnace

Want a quick way to determine whether the wire you're working with is the common #14 or #12? Pull out loose change; #14 wire is roughly the thickness of a dime, while #12 is the thickness of a nickel.

For efficiency and safety, individual wires are bundled inside cables. There are many different types. Materials and building standards have evolved over time. That means the cable in your house may differ from others, depending on when the structure was built. In the 1940s, for instance, "knob and tube" wiring was common. That method of wiring is no longer acceptable because of the fire danger. Armored cable is another older version, with wires running inside a ribbed steel tube. This wiring was often ungrounded, so also unsafe by today's standards. The current norm is "NM cable," encasing wires inside a paper sheath and a PVC outer shell color-coded by gauge.

Safety at Home

Electricity is unforgiving. Here are guidelines for keeping electricity flowing in the wires rather than through your skin.

- Always check any circuit with a tester, to ensure there is no voltage, before beginning work.

- Never drill or cut blind into a wall, ceiling, or floor. Check if there is electrical wiring behind the surface.

- Never change a plug to fit into an outlet (such as clipping off the third prong) or change an outlet to accept a plug.

- If you don't understand wiring you expose, stop and consult an electrician before proceeding. Damage to any one area can not only cause harm but can disrupt the house's entire electrical system.

- Never substitute electrical tape for a proper connection. Wire-to-wire connections should be made with the correct size wire nut (see page 103).

How to Strip NM Cable

TIME: 5 minutes / **SKILL LEVEL:** Easy

Growing skills and tackling increasingly complex household electrical projects inevitably means stripping NM cable. This has to be done correctly to avoid damaging wires.

What You'll Need

- Tape measure
- Cable ripper
- Multipurpose electrician's tool

How You Do It

1. Measure and mark the cable about 7" from the end. Slide the cable ripper onto the end and squeeze it to pierce the cable. Holding the tool closed, pull it toward the end and off, slicing the cable open.

2. Peel back the PVC sheathing and separate the paper inner layer from the wiring. Cut off extra sheathing and paper with the multipurpose tool.

3. Cut the wires to length (leave a minimum of 3" into an electrical box). Strip each wire using the correct opening on the multipurpose tool.

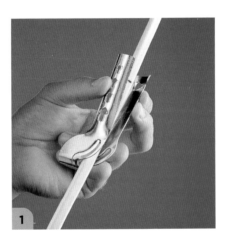

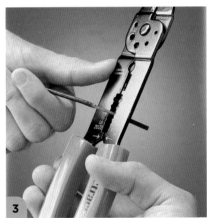

Work with Wires

TIME: 5 minutes / **SKILL LEVEL:** Easy

Working with electrical wires requires attention to detail. These are simple techniques, but do them wrong and you risk fire, electrical shorts, and shocks. The basic skills here are a foundation on which you can build other electrical skills.

What You'll Need

- Circuit tester
- Multipurpose electrician's tool
- Needle-nose pliers
- Linesman's pliers

How You Do It

1. For all these steps, turn the power off at the breaker box and check connections with a circuit tester to ensure they are not live. To connect wires to terminals or to each other, start by stripping about ¾" of the insulation from the end, using a multipurpose electrician's tool. Use the opening that matches the wire gauge, clamp down, and pull off the insulation.

2. Attach the wire to a receptacle terminal by forming a C-shaped hook in the stripped end using needle-nose pliers. Hook the wire around the screw terminal counterclockwise. The insulation should butt the screw so that no unsheathed wire projects from the terminal. If the bare section is too long, cut it and form the hook again. Never screw two wires to the same terminal.

3. Join wires by stripping the ends and holding the wire ends together and parallel to one another. Twist the ends with linesman's pliers, twisting three times to intertwine the ends.

4. Twist on a correct size wire connector (see page 103). Hand tighten the connector as far as it will go; no bare wire should run beyond the connector.

5. Pigtailing is mandated by electrical codes to attach two wires to the same terminal. This involves connecting two wires to a third, and then attach the third wire to the terminal. Start by cutting a 6" length of wire that is the same gauge and color of the wires you're pigtailing. Strip ¾" of the insulation from each end.

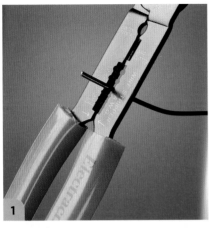

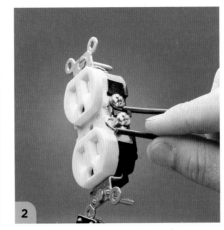

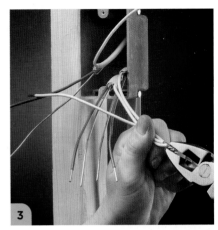

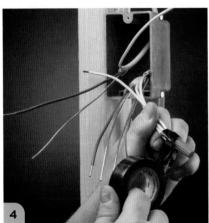

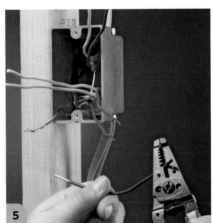

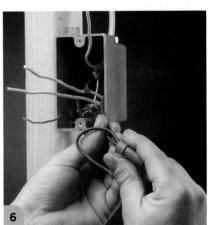

6. Twist together and connect one end of the pigtail to both free ends of the wires, securing the connection with the proper size of wire nut.

7. Connect the opposite end of the pigtail wire to the terminal. Check that all connections are secure before pushing the wires into the box and closing it up.

Install a Dimmer Switch

TIME: 20 minutes / **SKILL LEVEL:** Moderate

Replace a standard light switch with a dimmer switch to increase your control over the lighting in any room. This is a good project for the inexperienced DIYer to become familiar with basic electrical switch principles. Where the light is controlled by one wall switch, you'll buy a single-pole dimmer switch. If the light can be controlled from two different switches, you'll use a three-way dimmer switch to replace one of the switches (this project describes installing the more common single pole).

There must be enough room for the larger dimmer switch body in the existing electrical box. If the dimmer switch body doesn't fit, you'll need to replace the box. Most incandescent fixtures can be controlled by a standard dimmer. Compact fluorescent (CFL) and LED lights may not be dimmable; if they are, the dimmer must be made specifically for those bulbs. You'll also choose a traditional light switch with slider, a toggle switch, a dial, or slide action.

What You'll Need

- Phillips screwdriver
- Standard screwdriver
- Circuit tester
- Multipurpose electrician's tool
- Needle-nose pliers
- Dimmer switch
- Wire nuts

How You Do It

1. Turn off the power at the breaker. Unscrew and remove the existing cover plate. Use a circuit tester to confirm the power is off.

2. Unscrew the existing switch. Unscrew the wires from the switch terminals. Trim and strip the wire ends as needed, using a multipurpose electrician's tool and needle-nose pliers as necessary.

3. Connect the electrical box ground to the dimmer switch. Connect the red or live wire in the box to either black wire on the dimmer. Connect the second black wire to black or neutral box wire. Use wire nuts to secure all the wire connections. *Optional:* There is a slight difference in connecting a three-way dimmer switch. In removing the switch, note the wire connected to the switch's black screw—that is the live wire. Mark it. Disconnect all the wires and then connect the three-way dimmer switch by connecting the ground to ground, the two "traveler" wires inside the box to the two traveler wires (the non-live wires) from the switch. Connect the live wire from the switch to the live wire you marked.

4. Push the wires into the box and screw the dimmer switch in place. Turn the power back on and dim the lights fully and then brighten them again. If everything is okay, screw the new cover plate over the switch.

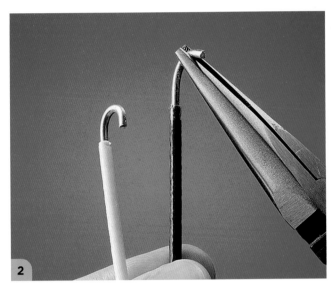

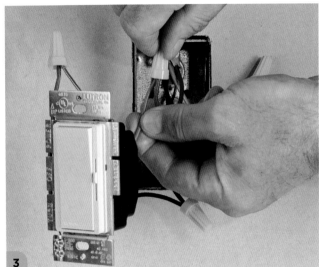

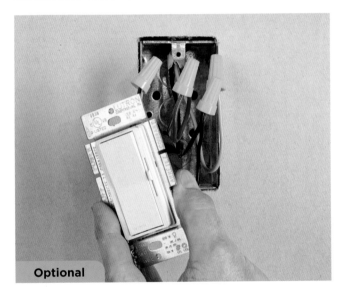

Optional

Install Raceway Conduit

TIME: 90 minutes / **SKILL LEVEL:** Moderate

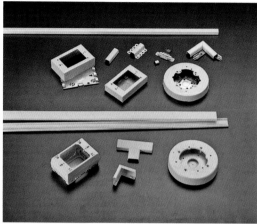

Raceway is metal channel used to carry wires on a wall rather than behind it. This can be a convenient wiring solution where you don't want to open a wall and modify studs to run wiring from one area to another. It doesn't necessarily have to carry bare wires; raceway conduit can also be a way to neatly route cables from a wall outlet plug to a wall-mounted TV or entertainment system. The conduit can be painted to match a wall or left beige or white. Raceway parts include two-part channels, corners and Ts, electrical and fixture boxes, and mounting hardware. (This project details a basic and common installation connecting start and end receptacle boxes with straight conduit and two elbow connectors.) Pieces are available in metal or plastic—although metal is preferred by most homeowners. Keep in mind that raceway conduit is not permissible in every situation. For instance, codes prohibit its use in areas that experience excessive moisture, such as bathrooms. Your local codes may also restrict raceway usage in other situations; always check with your local building department before installing it.

What You'll Need

- Tape measure
- Raceway conduit, electrical boxes, elbows, and hardware
- Circuit tester
- Phillips screwdriver
- Power drill and bits
- Stud finder
- Pencil
- Hacksaw
- Level
- Multipurpose electrician's tool
- Rubber mallet

How You Do It

1. Calculate the capacity of the circuit you're cutting into (see page 112). Measure from the host receptacle to the new fixture location. If you're splicing into the receptacle, you'll need a surface-mounted electrical box to start, raceway channel with any corners or intersections, and a surface-mounted fixture or electrical box to complete the extension (for plugs and cables, you only need the raceway). Add 10 percent to the length.

2. Shut off power to the circuit at the breaker box. Test the receptacle with a circuit tester to ensure power is off. Unscrew the faceplate and receptacle from the electrical box. Screw the raceway receptacle box (the "starter box") mounting plate to the existing electrical box.

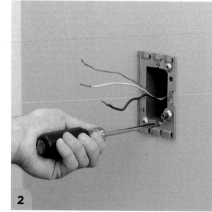

2

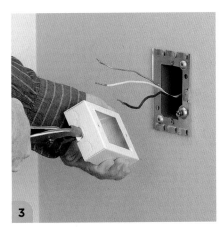

3

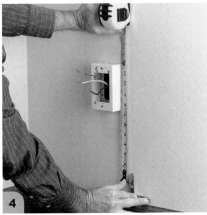

4

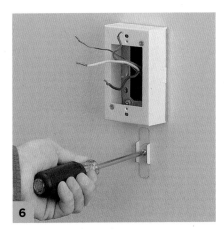

6

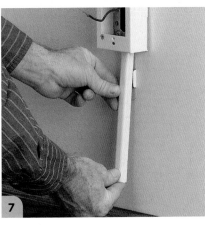

7

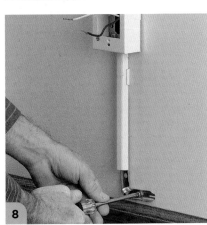

8

9

3. Remove the starter box knockout for the conduit. If there is more than one knockout outline, check the size and profile of your raceway and remove the knockout to match.

4. Screw the starter box to the mounting plate. Starting at the knockout in the starter box, measure from the box to the nearest junction you'll have to make with the conduit (usually an L turn requiring an elbow). If the connector runs right above the baseboard, leave ¼" gap between the two. Screw the connector mounting plate to the wall.

5. Determine the new receptacle box location; it should be attached to a stud, if possible. Drill pilot holes and screw the mounting plate in place. *Optional:* If you're simply running cables to a wall-mounted TV, you'll terminate the conduit without a receptacle box. In that case, end the run with a mounting clip (see step 6).

6. Use a stud finder to locate studs between the two receptacle boxes. Use a pencil to mark the locations and screw mounting clips to the wall at the stud locations, keeping the clips ¼" from any baseboard, molding, or adjacent wall. Screw mounting clips into place ½" under the knockouts on both receptacle boxes.

7. Measure and use a hacksaw to cut a short section of raceway to extend from the first receptacle box to the elbow. Snap it into the clip and repeat the process at the opposite receptacle box.

8. Position an elbow mounting plate directly below the track from the receptacle box, checking that the bottom horizontal leg is level. Screw it in place and repeat for the opposite receptacle box.

9. Measure between the elbow leg ends and cut the track to match. Snap the track onto the mounting brackets and elbows, tapping with a mallet as needed. If track is longer than the length you buy, use two sections butted together at a mounting bracket and covered with a straight connector.

(continued) ▶

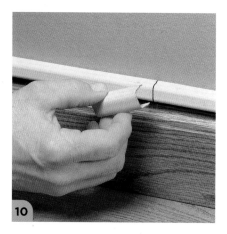

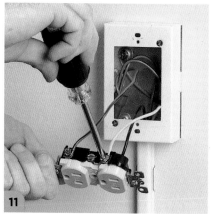

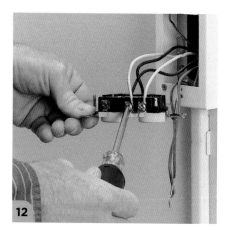

10. Cut black, white, and green THNN wire 2' longer than the distance box to box. Snake the wire ends into the starter box, down into the track, all the way to the end box. Pull out about 1' of wire.

11. Snap the elbow covers on the track, tapping with a mallet to seat them. Starting with the new receptacle, strip the wire ends as necessary and attach the black wire to the receptacle's hot terminal (usually a gold screw). Connect the white to the silver screw, and the green to the ground or green screw. Tuck the wire cluster into the receptacle box and screw the receptacle to the face of the box.

12. At the starter box, screw the opposite ends of the black and white wires opposite each other on the gold and silver screws, as on the end receptacle. Connect the house black and white wires on the screws right above the wires you just attached.

13. Cut a 6" piece of green wire and strip both ends (this will be the "pigtail"). Twist one end of the pigtail with the ground wire ends (usually green and bare copper) in the box, covering with the correct size wire nut. Connect the other end of the pigtail to the receptacle's ground screw.

14. Tuck the wires into the box and screw the receptacle onto the face of the box. Turn the power back on and check all outlets. Screw the cover plates over the receptacles on each end.

Calculating Circuit Capacity

Each breaker in your box represents a circuit. The total electrical capacity of a circuit is a simple calculation: the amps for which the circuit is rated, times the voltage for that circuit (usually 120 volts). So, for instance, a typical circuit might have a 15-amp breaker, so the capacity is 15 amps × 120 volts = 1,800 watts. That's total capacity; electrical pros generally consider 20 percent less the "safe operating capacity" (so, in this case, 1,440 watts). Once you know the circuit capacity, add up the wattage of fixtures and appliances on the circuit. That number cannot exceed max capacity of the circuit. Wattages are listed on the fixture or appliance.

Upgrade an Outlet to GFCI

TIME: 15 minutes / **SKILL LEVEL:** Moderate

GFCI (ground fault circuit interrupter) outlets are a modern safety feature that are now an integral part of building codes. These are used primarily where moisture is a constant—in rooms such as kitchens, bathrooms, and laundry rooms. The GFCI is designed to react amazingly quickly to small changes in current, shutting off the circuit and preventing fire and injury. If you own an older home, it's wise to replace bathroom and kitchen outlets with GFCI versions. Be aware that the outlets are bigger than standard electrical outlets and may not fit into older, smaller electrical boxes. In those cases, upgrade the box as well as the receptacle.

How You Do It

1. Turn the power off at the breaker box. Unscrew and remove the cover plate and the receptacle. Use a circuit tester to double-check that the power is off.

2. Disconnect the wires from the existing receptacle. Reattach them to the same terminals on the GFCI receptacle (the hot terminal will normally be labeled "hot line"). Connect the copper ground wire to the green terminal. *Optional:* If there are more than one white and one black wire, cut 6" pieces of white and black wires (pigtails) and strip each end. Twist the ends of the white wires together with one end of the white pigtail and secure it with the correct size wire nut. Connect it to the neutral, silver terminal. Repeat the process with the black wires and pigtail, connecting the pigtail to the hot line terminal on the GFCI. Connect the copper ground to the green terminal.

3. Tuck the wiring back into the electrical box and screw the GFCI to the front of the box. Turn the power back on and test the GFCI, following to the manufacturer's directions. Screw on the GFCI faceplate.

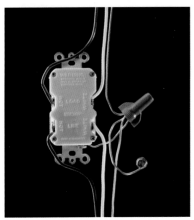

Wire connections for GFCI outlets

What You'll Need

- Phillips screwdriver
- Circuit tester
- GFCI receptacle
- Multipurpose electrician's tool
- Wire nuts (optional)
- Wire (optional)

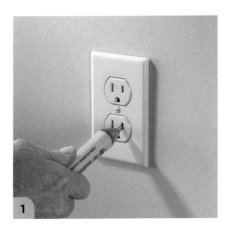

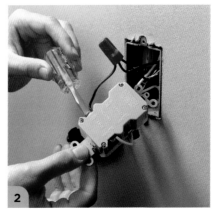

Install a Whole-House Surge Protector

TIME: 1 hour / **SKILL LEVEL:** Challenging

The worst thing that can happen to a residential electrical system is a surge of power. Where a surge of water pressure might just cause a burst pipe or leak, the surge from something as simple as a lightning strike to a local power transformer can cause widespread havoc in your home's electrical system, even destroying or damaging expensive electronics and key fixtures. Lightning strikes aren't the only cause; power surges can result from auto accidents involving local grid equipment, sudden changes in power patterns, and other malfunctions. As awful as a catastrophic surge might be, the same damage can happen on a smaller scale with micro surges lasting a second or less and going unnoticed. Those can cause mysterious electronic failures and shorten appliance life span. A whole-house surge protector ensures against that damage.

Unlike power-strip surge protectors, which can be overwhelmed and fail when you need them the most, a whole-house protector is wired where the electricity enters the house. The two basic types are units installed at the meter by a professional electrician and an interior protector wired into the breaker box. (This project describes installing the latter.) Regardless of which you choose, whole-house surge protectors should be labeled with the Underwriters Laboratories (UL) 1449 rating.

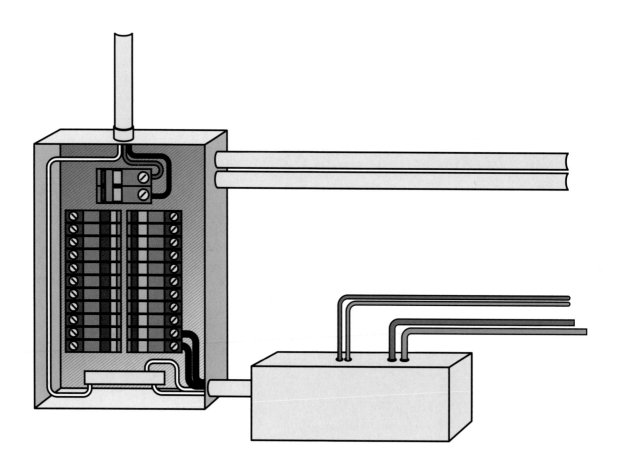

What You'll Need

- Circuit tester
- Screwdriver
- Whole-house surge protector
- Hammer
- Multipurpose electrician's tool
- (2) 15-amp single-pole breakers

How You Do It

1. Turn off power at the power main and remove the breaker box cover. Check each breaker with a circuit tester to ensure there is no power. Decide on the best position for the surge protector unit. Typically, the protector box is mounted with its nipple aligned with a breaker box side knockout. The protector has screw flanges, allowing it to be fastened to a wall. However, they vary in construction; follow the manufacturer's instructions.

2. Remove the breaker box knockout (tap it out with a hammer). Screw the protector box to the wall, with the nipple end to the knockout and the wires running through. Route the protector's wires to reach the breaker box slots in as efficient a route as possible. Trim and strip the ends. Connect the black wires to two dedicated 15-amp breakers.

3. Connect the protector's white wire to the breaker box's white neutral bar. Connect the green wire to the ground bar. Snap the two breakers into the lowest terminal bar slots.

4. Turn the power on. Use a circuit tester with a readout to check that the voltage between the two black protector leads is 240 volts. Replace the breaker box cover. Check that the indicator lights on the protector are lit.

Install Under-Cabinet Lighting

TIME: 45 minutes / **SKILL LEVEL:** Easy

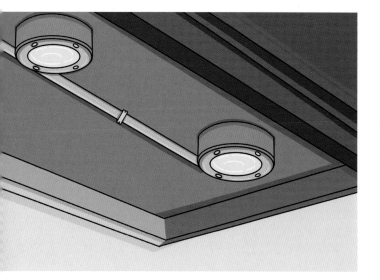

Kitchen under-cabinet lighting affects both safety and aesthetics. Illuminating a typically shadowed area allows you to more safely cut and prepare food. It also adds a welcoming brightness to a room where abundant light is equated with cleanliness.

You can install battery-operated fixtures, but they are cumbersome and it's hard to fully conceal the fixtures or battery pack. Individual plug-in lights are an option, but using more than one leads to cord clutter that gets in the way of kitchen functions. Some homeowners hardwire under-cabinet lighting into the nearest circuit. That is a big undertaking and requires opening the wall and in-depth electrical work. A happy medium is low-voltage under-cabinet lighting. A single plug powers a series of fixtures, and installation requires modest time and effort.

Choose between strip fixtures and pucks (pucks are shown here, but strips are installed in a similar manner). Strips offer more even illumination. They are great for adding ambient light. Puck spotlights are a more dramatic and contemporary look, ideal for task lighting where you prepare food. You'll likely come across tape lights as well. These provide accent lighting and aren't usually used to illuminate work surfaces. They are placed in toe-kick recesses or on top of cabinets.

What You'll Need

- Tape measure
- Under-cabinet puck lights
- Pencil
- Power drill and bits
- Hole saw (optional)
- Screwdriver
- Hammer
- Cable clips

How You Do It

1. Measure your cabinets' bottom lip before you buy the lights to ensure fixtures and power hub will be concealed. Clear off the countertop.

2. Lay out the lights and cords on the counter underneath the cabinets to determine where the individual fixtures will go (most manufacturers recommend spacing lights at least 12" apart). The power cord must be able to reach an outlet.

3. Measure and mark each puck location on the cabinet bottoms. They should be 1" or less from the front lip. Drill an access hole to the nearest outlet inside the cabinet (if there isn't one, skip this and use a wall outlet).

Optional: If your cabinets have no bottom lip and you want to recess the pucks, drill holes in the cabinet bottoms at each location, using a hole saw. Snap each fixture out of its housing, feed the wires through the hole, and screw the puck to the bottom.

4. Remove the lens from the base of the first puck. Position the base and mark for the screws. Drill shallow pilot holes being careful not to drill all the way through. Screw the fixture in place—wire notch facing to the back—using the screws provided.

5. Repeat with the remaining pucks. Use cable clips to secure the wires to the cabinet bottoms, out of sight. Mount the light switch on a cabinet side or wall. Plug the transformer and power supply into the nearest outlet. Test the lights and fix connections as necessary. Attach the lens covers over each puck.

Replace a Ceiling Light Fixture

TIME: 30 minutes / **SKILL LEVEL:** Moderate

Swapping out an old ceiling light fixture for a newer model can go a long way toward changing the look of the room. It's also a way to increase the available light or even change the light type—such as going from the warm yellow of an incandescent fixture to the sparkling blue of an LED or halogen.

What You'll Need

- Circuit tester
- New lighting fixture
- Multipurpose electrician's tool
- Screwdriver

How You Do It

1. Shut off power to the room at the breaker box. Remove the shade and loosen the fixture base mounting screws. Remove the base and hold it (or have a helper hold it). Check the connections with a circuit tester to ensure the power is off to the fixture, and then unscrew the wire nuts from the existing connections.

2. Check that the ceiling box is UL approved and up to code. If it isn't, replace it. Cut off the ends of the wires with a multipurpose tool. Strip about ³/₄" at the end of each wire.

3. If there is not a structurally sound mounting strap in place, install one. (Some light fixtures are sold with mounting straps. If so, install the mounting strap that came with the fixture.)

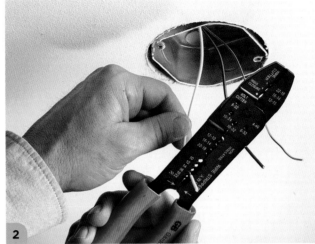

4. Screw the electrical box ground and the fixture ground to the mounting strap ground screw. (You'll need to hold the fixture base plate up or have a helper do it.) If the manufacturer specifies a different ground method or wiring diagram, follow the manufacturer's instructions.

5. Connect the electrical box white wire with the fixture's white wire, and black to black, using the correct size wire nut.

6. Screw the fixture's base plate to the mounting bracket or screw the fixture's threaded nipple into the female threaded opening. Put a bulb in the fixture and turn the power on. Test that the light works and then put any remaining bulbs in the fixture and fasten the shade or cover.

Replace a Ceiling Fixture with Track Lighting

TIME: 45 minutes / **SKILL LEVEL:** Moderate

Track lighting remains a popular upgrade for homeowners. Whereas a single overhead fixture may not serve the room well, track lighting allows you to point the light exactly where you need it to go. Choose between LED and halogen fixtures to control the lighting color and brightness. There are also a wealth of options when it comes to style—from units that visually fade into the ceiling and nearly disappear to funky, fun, and artistic versions that make a style statement all by themselves. In any case, this is an easy upgrade, although a helper will make the project much easier and more manageable.

What You'll Need

- Track lighting
- Phillips screwdriver
- Circuit tester
- Measuring tape
- Pencil
- Hacksaw (optional)
- Power drill and bits
- Stud finder
- Toggle or molly bolt (optional)
- Multipurpose electrician's tool
- Wire nuts

How You Do It

1. Turn off power to the light fixture at the breaker box. Unbox the new track lighting and check that all pieces and hardware have been included. Remove the existing shade and bulbs. Unscrew the base from the mounting bracket.

2. Use a circuit tester to double-check that the power is off. Disconnect the electrical box wires from the existing fixture and remove the fixture.

3. Pull the box wiring through the hole in the track lighting mounting bracket. Screw the bracket to the electrical box. Fasten the green or copper house ground wire to the green ground screw on the strap. *Optional:* Measure and mark the track to the length desired. If necessary, wrap tape at the mark and cut the track to length with a hacksaw. If your lighting comes with more than one piece, assemble the connections and any T- or L-fittings that you might be using (to create a layout different than the standard straight run).

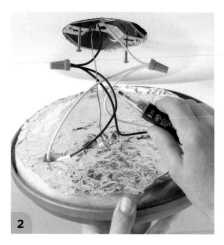

2

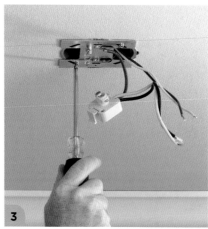

3

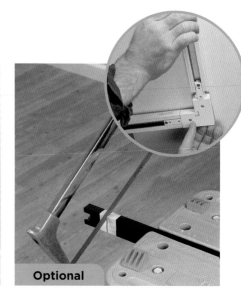

Optional

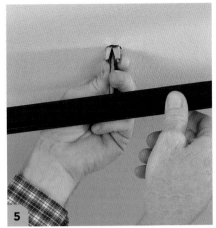

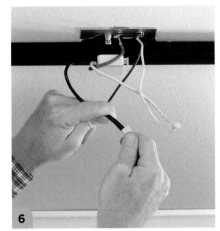

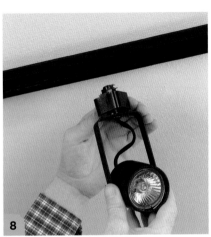

4. Place the track in the mounting bracket saddle. Mark mounting hole locations on the ceiling with a pencil (if your track does not have predrilled mounting holes, drill ³/₁₆" holes every 12" to 14" and mark these locations on the ceiling).

5. Mark joist locations with a stud finder. Screws can be driven directly through the mounting holes at these locations. Otherwise, slip a toggle or molly bolt through the track mounting holes and drill ⁵/₈" access holes at the marked points on the ceiling. Hold the track up and push the bolts into the access holes far enough to expand the wings. Tighten the bolts until the track is snug against the ceiling.

6. Strip as necessary with a multipurpose electrician's tool and connect the house wires to the track's power supply fitting wires: black to black, and white to white. Use the correct size wire nuts to secure the connections. (The ground wire from the track's power supply is usually pigtailed to the electrical box's ground and connected to the mounting bracket ground screw. Follow the manufacturer's directions.)

7. Tuck the wiring into the track mount cover and snap or screw it in place. Cap the track ends with dead-end cap fittings.

8. Insert the heads into the track (usually by slipping the stem in and twisting). Make sure each head is secure before letting go. Slide and point the light heads where you want them. Turn on the power and test the lights.

5. Interior Surfaces

Thanks to the sheer visual space they take up, the surfaces in a house determine the overall style and feel of the interior more than any other feature. Dingy or damaged surfaces have just as powerful a negative impact. The good news? Sprucing up or repairing interior surfaces are some of the easiest, most satisfying, and best skill-building projects a homeowner can tackle. As a bonus, they are also some of the biggest bang-for-the-buck improvements you can make.

Surface repairs and upkeep are, however, an ongoing battle because the largest surfaces in your home take the most abuse. Just think how much mileage your living room floor sees, or how often you prepare food or drop things on a kitchen floor.

With that in mind, this chapter covers the most common surface mishaps and simple, easy, and rewarding improvements you can make to the surfaces in your house. The techniques you'll pick up will be useful throughout the house. Paint a room correctly and it will look significantly better than one that was painted sloppily—and you'll have the skill to paint every room in the house like a pro. Fix a squeaking wood floor in a bedroom and you can do the same thing to an old wood living room floor.

What's more, the skills you'll pick up from this chapter can easily be built on to successfully complete more ambitious and transformative home projects. It isn't much of a technical leap from installing a backsplash (page 132) to tiling a tub surround. Learn to put down laminate click-lock planks and you can do a similar floor in linoleum's cousin, Marmoleum.

Understanding Surface Construction

Almost every surface in a house, with the exception of solid-surface countertops, is built up in layers. Here are the basics of the surfaces you'll likely repair or improve.

- **Walls:** Some old houses have plaster walls that are created by layering plaster on thin wood "lath." These are subject to cracking and are best repaired or resurfaced by a professional. Most modern houses are constructed of drywall nailed or screwed to wall studs and ceiling joists.

- **Floors:** Surfaces underfoot are created with a plywood subfloor nailed to joists and covered with wood strips, resilient floor such as laminates or linoleum, hard tiles, or carpet. Carpet, wood, and resilient flooring are often installed over a soft "underlayment" that cushions the floor and makes it softer to walk on and less noisy.

- **Countertops:** Tiled countertops are the most prone

to breakage or problems with water infiltration, with "post-form" types a close second because they have seams. Solid counters, such as quartz, stone, recycled glass, or solid-surface materials, can endure a lot of abuse without showing damage. However, care and cleaning are essential to keeping these surfaces looking as nice as possible (see page 136).

Drywall covers most house walls and ceilings. It comes in standard panels 4' wide by 8' long (12' and 16' lengths are available but rarely used by homeowners). The panels are ¼", ⅜", ½", or ⅝" thick.

Special drywall called "greenboard" is used in areas where moisture is an issue. Different types are used in different applications, as backer to tile or paint in bathrooms and kitchens.

Wood floors, such as this wide-plank surface, shout luxury—but only when properly maintained.

Paint an Interior Correctly

TIME: 45 minutes (depending on surface area and prep needed) / **SKILL LEVEL:** Easy

Painting is the most basic and useful of DIY skills. Because the techniques are so straightforward, DIYers often make the mistake of thinking they were born knowing how to paint. But there is a right and a wrong way to paint surfaces. The difference between a professional quality job and sloppy, amateurish work is painfully apparent. Keep in mind that any painting project is something you'll see and live with on a daily basis. It pays to take your time and do it right. Do a good job and interior painting is the closest you'll come to instantaneous gratification. The right wall color transforms a space and freshens the space.

Start by understanding how paint and light interact. An uneven top coat allows light to reflect differently from one area to the next. That creates a spotty, unattractive look, as do roller or brush marks. A too-thin top coat allows the underlying color, whatever it was, to influence how the eye reads the final color. Prevent these problems because they are nearly impossible to fix after painting, except by completely repainting. That's why the most useful painting tools are patience and attention to detail. Small details make a big difference, and even a small error can stand out like a sore thumb.

Money Wise

Bargain paints often aren't. Off-brand products tend to be thinner, taking more coats to cover and costing more in the long run because you have to use more paint to get the same coverage. Similarly, tints may not be as true to the color swatches as they are with expensive brands. Always sample any paint and buy carefully, checking online reviews from other customers.

SkillBuilder

Proper "cut-in" around the borders of a surface is essential to a polished, professional result. Getting it right means developing your brush-handling expertise and avoiding common mistakes. The guidelines below will help you do just that.

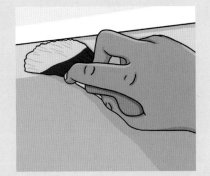

- **Use an angled sash brush.** These are much more efficient and easier to control when cutting in and are perfect for getting into corners.

- **Work from a paint pail, rather than a full bucket of paint,** to increase your control and reduce the likelihood of spills.

- **Don't overload the brush.** It's better to apply a second coat, than to lay down a thick coat that ends up running, dripping, or bleeding under tape seams.

- **Work in the brightest light possible.** It can be difficult to see where a lighter top coat is going over primer. Bright light makes the separation clearer.

- **Learn to freehand.** Pros rarely tape seams. You can save a lot of time and hassle by learning to cut in as they do. (Practice on taped-off surfaces). Drag the brush parallel to the adjacent surface. On the first pass, leave a ⅛" gap. Fill in the gap on your second pass.

- **Cut a trough on textured ceilings.** Use a putty knife to cut a very thin (⅛" or less) valley along the edge of a textured ceiling at the seam. As you cut in, the paint will flow into and be contained by this "trough."

What You'll Need

- Drop cloths
- Spackling compound
- 220-grit sandpaper or sanding sponge
- Sponge
- Paint
- Putty knife
- Wood putty
- TSP (optional)
- Bucket (optional)
- Painter's tape
- Primer
- 2" paintbrush
- Roller set
- Telescoping roller handle

How You Do It

1. Spread drop cloths to protect floors and furniture. Prep cracks, holes, or other damage by filling with spackle, letting it dry, and sanding smooth. Wipe the wall clean of any dust with a damp sponge. For significant drywall damage, see pages 128 and 129. Fill defects in wood trim with wood putty and sand smooth. *Optional:* Wash extremely dirty walls or trim with a mild soap-and-water solution. For stubborn grime, use trisodium phosphate (TSP) following the directions on the box. If you are painting a room in an older house and suspect the existing paint contains lead, test it using a test kit (available at home centers).

(continued) ▶

2. Use painter's tape to protect seams at baseboards, flooring, trim, or any area you don't intend to paint. Apply short strips, generously overlapped. Finish by dragging a putty knife blade over the seam to ensure the tape is sealed.

3. Cut in with primer, brushing a 3" band along joints between surfaces. Roll the surface before the cut-in dries. Roll 3' × 3' sections, starting on the ceiling and working out from one corner. Use a telescoping roller handle rather than a ladder.

4. Prime a wall working in 3' × 4' sections (two sections top to bottom), working from one edge and from top to bottom. To ensure complete coverage, roll an overlapping "W" pattern. *Pro Tip:* Although white primer is the norm, you can have the store tint the primer to match the top coat color, to ensure against show-through.

5. Once dry, check the surface for blobs, ridges, or imperfections. Sand any you find. Wipe off sanding dust with a moist sponge.

6. Open the paint can and stir it with a stir stick. You can use a drill with a paddle mixer attachment to mix larger, 5-gallon buckets of paint, but avoid splashes. *Optional:* If you're painting several walls or a big room, "box" multiple gallons of paint, combining paint into one large container (such as a 5-gallon bucket). Slowly and steadily stir the paint until it is a uniform color. This prevents color variations wall to wall.

7. Cut in one wall at a time, so that the paint is still wet when you roll it. Roll the wall in the same way you primed it. Work quickly so that no part of the surface dries before you're finished.

8. Finish painting the walls. Remove the painter's tape as soon as the paint starts to set up and becomes tacky but before it dries entirely.

9. Once the wall paint is dry, tape off any trim that will be painted. A 2" brush is usually best for trim. Work from the top down on windows and doors, and from the frame into the sash or door.

Pro Tip

Accent walls—a small portion of the room, painted in a much bolder or contrasting color—are not as in vogue as they once were but can still be a way to introduce vibrant color into an otherwise subtle look. Accent walls draw attention, so be absolutely precise when painting one. Carefully tape off adjacent surfaces so the borders are crisp and allow the accent wall to pop exactly as you want it to.

Repair Drywall Nail Pops

TIME: 20 minutes (depending on number of pops) / **SKILL LEVEL:** Easy

Drywall in older homes may have been installed with nails rather than screws. Over time, the nails work themselves out and create "nail pops"—small, unattractive blemishes in the surface. Fix all of them at the same time.

What You'll Need

- Power drill and bits, or driver
- 2" drywall screws
- Hammer
- Spackle
- Putty knife
- Sandpaper or sanding sponge
- Primer and paint
- 1" paintbrush

How You Do It

1. Drive a drywall screw into the wall 1" right above the nail pop. Carefully hammer the nail pop flush. Spackle over both. Let dry, sand the repair, and prime and paint the wall.

Pro Tip

Fix small holes with drywall supplies on hand or go the easier route and buy a drywall patch kit. These include a self-adhesive screen patch, a small tub of compound, and a plastic putty knife. Stick the patch over the hole, cover with compound in a crisscross pattern, smooth, and feather the edges. Let dry, sand, prime, and paint the wall.

Fix a Medium Drywall Hole or Crack

TIME: 30 minutes / **SKILL LEVEL:** Easy

A door slamming open or even moving furniture can create a hole too large for a patch kit. In that case, apply what is known as a "California patch."

What You'll Need

- Tape measure
- Pencil
- Metal straightedge
- 2' × 2' drywall repair panel
- Utility knife
- Speed square or carpenter's square
- Drywall saw
- Putty knife
- Wall compound
- Sandpaper or sanding sponge
- Primer and paint
- Paintbrush

How You Do It

1. Measure and mark the drywall for a square patch at least 2" larger on all sides than the hole, using a metal straightedge. Measure and score the back of the drywall with a smaller square, 1 ½" smaller on all sides. Snap off the rectangular gypsum section on each side, and carefully peel off the face paper.

2. Hold the patch over the hole and mark around the gypsum center (not including the paper-only lip). Use a drywall saw to cut out the square around the hole.

3. Coat the patch's paper border with wall compound. Stick the patch in place and spread compound over it. Smooth and feather into the surrounding surface. Sand and apply a second coat, if necessary. Sand smooth, prime, and paint the wall.

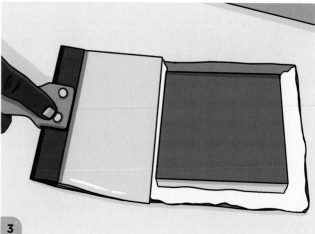

●●○

Repair a Large Drywall Hole

TIME: 45 minutes / **SKILL LEVEL:** Moderate

Drywall patches for larger holes need to be secured in place to be stable and long lasting. That means creating a surface to which the patch can be screwed.

What You'll Need

- Tape measure
- Pencil
- Drywall
- Utility knife
- Metal straightedge
- Drywall saw
- 1" × 2" scrap pieces
- 2" deck screws
- Putty knife
- Joint tape
- Wall compound
- Sandpaper or sanding sponge
- Primer and paint
- Paintbrush

How You Do It

1. Measure and mark the drywall for a square patch 1" larger on all sides than the damaged section. Score cut lines on the drywall surface with a utility knife. Snap the patch out.

2. Hold the patch in front of the damaged area and mark the outline with a pencil. Use a drywall saw to cut out the marked area.

3. Cut two 1" × 2" scraps about 3" longer than the patch. Slip one into the hole in the wall and screw it along and just inside one edge with 2" deck screws. Repeat with the second piece along the opposite edge.

4. Place the patch into the wall and screw it to the wood strips. Line the seams with joint tape and cover with a layer of compound. Smooth and feather the edges into the surrounding surface.

5. Sand and apply a second coat, if needed. Sand smooth, prime, and paint the wall.

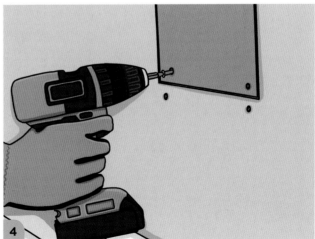

Repair a Damaged Wall Corner

TIME: 1 hour / **SKILL LEVEL:** Moderate

A crumpled wall corner is an eyesore in any room. It can also seem like a challenge to fix, but not when you have the right know-how and some basic tools.

What You'll Need

- Drop cloth
- Utility knife
- Putty knife
- Hacksaw
- Pry bar
- Aviation snips
- Corner bead
- Drywall nails
- Hammer
- Drywall compound
- Small taping knife
- Sandpaper or sanding sponge
- Primer and paint
- Paintbrush

How You Do It

1. Lay a drop cloth under the work area. Mark and score a rectangle around the top, sides, and bottom of the damage. Cut into the edges of the damaged corner bead with a utility knife. Clean out the old compound covering the corner bead with a stiff putty knife so that the corner bead is completely exposed.

2. Use a hacksaw to cut along the scored marks top and bottom. Use a pry bar to remove the damaged section. Use aviation snips to cut a new section to match the old. *Optional:* If the damaged section terminates at the bottom or top of the wall, cut the end so that it doesn't overlap with existing corner bead. Mark and cut each side of one end to a 45° angle before proceeding.

3. Nail the new corner bead in place. Cover with two or three coats of compound, using a small taping knife (sand between coats). Feather the top coat into the surrounding surface and sand to create a crisp, sharp edge. Prime and paint.

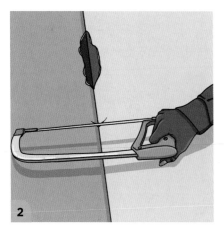

2

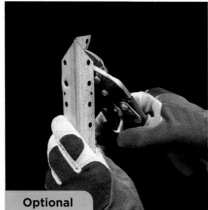

Optional

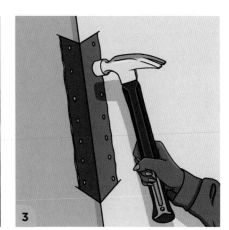

3

Hang a Floating Shelf

TIME: 20 minutes / **SKILL LEVEL:** Easy

A floating shelf is an interesting look and useful addition to any room. It's easy to install and great where a more substantial solution such as bracket shelving would be hard to position or install. Floating shelves are, however, limited in the weight they can support; so it's important to read and follow the manufacturer's warnings. They're ideal for the bathroom or for a spice shelf in a kitchen. The glass shelf here is a bit of a hybrid, installed as other floating shelves are, but with decorative support escutcheons. The supports for most floating shelves are completely concealed.

What You'll Need

- Shelf
- Tape measure
- Stud finder (optional)
- Pencil
- Level
- Drill

How You Do It

1. Assemble the shelf as necessary. Some require bracket receivers be screwed into cutouts in the shelf's back edge; the shelf here is fit with decorative brackets prior to hanging. Hold the shelf in position and mark the center point of each bracket. *Optional:* Adjust shelf location for shelves that will hold extra weight by using a stud finder so that the supports can be screwed into studs.

2. Use a level to mark 3" vertical lines at the marks. Use the level to mark across the lines for the center of the brackets.

3. Center the bracket on the intersection of the lines. Mark and drill a pilot hole for the mounting bracket screw. Use a screw anchor or screw directly into studs. Screw the mounting brackets to the wall.

4. Slip the shelf brackets onto the mounting brackets and tighten the setscrew to secure them. Check level and slip the glass shelf into the shelf bracket on each side; adjust as necessary.

Install a Backsplash

TIME: 2 hours / **SKILL LEVEL:** Moderate

A backsplash adds undeniable flair to that often-too-bare wall between the countertop and the upper cabinets. A backsplash project is a wonderfully achievable project to prepare you for larger projects like tiling a bathroom floor. This will take one full Saturday or half of two weekend days.

This project uses grid mosaics—tiny square tiles attached to a square foot flexible vinyl mesh. It's a popular option for kitchens and baths because the tiles look appealing and installation is simplified (fewer tiles to position and cement to the wall). These products come in a stunning array, from glass tiles to ceramic mosaics and even stainless steel versions. There are also shapes such as hexagons and circles. Regardless, the process you'll use is the same for installing individual tiles except that you don't use spacers to ensure uniform spacing between tiles.

What You'll Need

- Backsplash tiles
- 1" × 2" story stick
- Tape measure
- Torpedo level
- Pencil
- Carpenter's level
- Painter's tape
- Notched trowel
- Mastic adhesive
- Masking tape (optional)
- Tile nippers
- 2×4 scrap
- Carpet or thick towel scrap
- Rubber mallet
- Grout
- Rubber grout float
- Sponge
- Clean soft cloth
- Caulk
- Drop cloth
- Caulk gun

How You Do It

1. Mark a 1" × 2" story stick that is at least half as long as the backsplash area. Measure and mark the stick with pencil marks representing the joints between the tile segments (in this case, 1' increments, but check against the actual tile sheets).

2. Measure and mark a vertical centerline on the backsplash (use a torpedo level). Use the story stick to mark tile unit placement. If an end piece would require an unusual cut, adjust the layout to accommodate the easiest fabrication and most attractive appearance (whole mosaic tiles look best; larger segments of mesh units work best).

3. Countertops are usually not perfectly level. Use a carpenter's level to find the lowest point of the counter and mark a full mosaic tile up from that point. Determine level from that point and measure up the distance of one complete mesh tile unit from the lower line. Mark an upper level line; this is the reference line for the top of the mesh segments.

4. Line the counter back edge with painter's tape. Trowel mastic onto the wall evenly, beneath the top reference line. Work in sections less than 4' long. Comb the surface with the trowel's notched edge.

5. Press the tiles into place, twisting them slightly as you align them with the reference lines. *Pro Tip:* If tiles seem heavy enough to pull away from the wall, tape them in place with masking tape until the mastic dries.

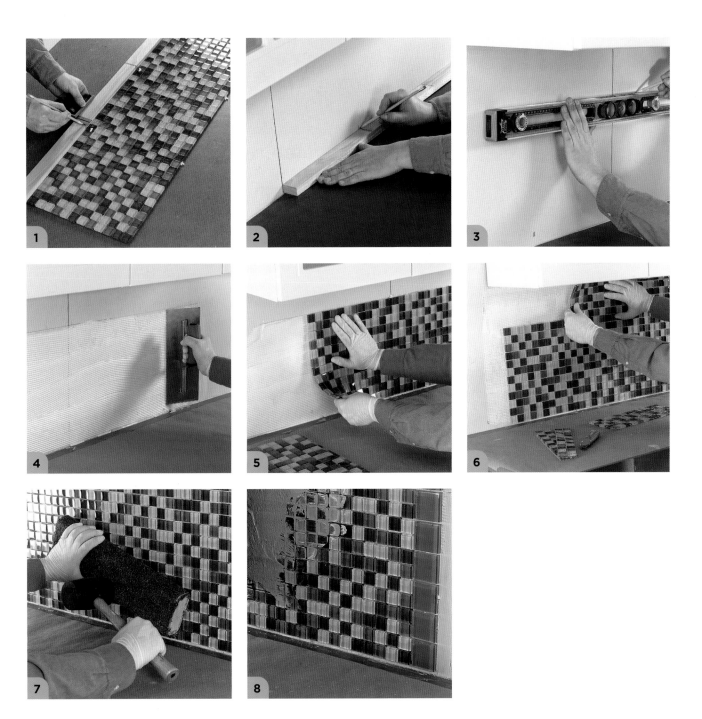

6. Finish installing the first row and then cut and install the top row if necessary.

7. Ensure the finished backsplash is securely seated by wrapping a 2×4 scrap in carpet scrap or a thick old towel and tapping with a rubber mallet. Let the mastic dry for 24 hours.

8. Mix the grout and spread it with the float kept at a 30° angle. Press the grout forcefully into the joints. Wipe off excess grout with the float, holding it at about a right angle. Work diagonally. *Pro Tip:* Use non-sanded grout for gaps thinner than ⅛".

9. Clean excess grout off the surface with a damp sponge. When the grout has largely dried, buff the surface clean with a soft cloth. After 24 hours, re-move the tape on the countertop and lay a bead of caulk between the backsplash and counter.

Wall-Mount a Flat-Screen TV

TIME: 45 minutes / **SKILL LEVEL:** Moderate

The modern flat-screen TV is a space-saver. You lose that benefit if you just stand it up on a console or in an entertainment center. Most manufacturers figured this out a long time ago, which is why you'll find aftermarket mounting kits for almost any flat-screen TV. Just match the size and make of the television to the mount.

What You'll Need

- TV mounting kit
- Tarp or drop cloth
- Soft, clean towel
- Phillips screwdriver
- LED screen cleaner
- Stud finder
- Tape measure
- Pencil
- Level
- Power drill and bits

How You Do It

1. Unbox the mounting kit and check that all hardware has been included. Use a tarp, drop cloth, or just a clean, empty area of countertop as a staging area. Make sure you have enough room to maneuver.

2. Lay the television facedown on a soft, clean surface such as a towel, blanket, or clean canvas drop cloth. Remove any feet or base. Screw the mounting brackets to the back of the TV.

3. Determine the height at which the TV will be mounted. Use a stud finder to locate and mark stud centers in the area. Measure and mark the wall where the bottom of the brackets will hang and mark the bracket mounting plate screw holes.

4. Hold the mounting plates in position and check level. Screw the mounting plates—usually a top and bottom plate—into studs on each end, using the screws supplied. Check level one final time. *Optional:* If you are concealing TV cables in the wall, cut openings behind where the TV will be positioned and near the bottom of the wall, where the electronic entertainment components will be placed. Run the cables from top to bottom and install wall plates as needed and required by code.

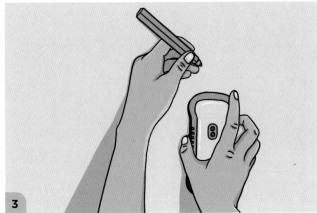

5. Hook the TV brackets onto the wall mounts (some have features that require the brackets be screwed to the mounts; follow the manufacturer's instructions). This will be much easier with a helper. Connect the TV to the entertainment system components and adjust the height as necessary. Clean the screen with a screen cleaner meant for your type of TV screen prior to turning the system and the TV on.

Optional: If you prefer not to run cables through the wall, but want to conceal them, use wall-mounted raceway conduit from the entertainment system components to the TV. See page 110 for installation instructions.

Pro Tip

Most homeowners hang wall-mounted TVs too high. The exact center of the screen should be level with a person's eyes when they are sitting on the couch. That measurement is usually 36" to 38" above the floor (remember, that's the center, not the bottom or top, of the TV). This is the position at which the TV is meant to be viewed to get the most out of your viewing experience. Add soft lighting behind the TV for a cinematic experience when watching movies.

Countertop Cleaning Guide

Not all countertops are created equal, but all countertops are the hardest-working, most abused surfaces in any home. Bathroom surfaces are exposed to many colorful health and beauty products, not to mention abundant moisture. Kitchen counters see the business end of cutlery and are subject to hot pots, staining food and drink, and more. Different countertop materials require different care, maintenance, and cleaning. Knowing the best way to clean your particular surfaces is key to keeping them looking lovely over time.

- **Laminates:** Some of the most common and inexpensive countertops, laminates are usually used in kitchens. Although modern laminates can mimic stone or wood surfaces, the material is less durable than other options.

  Care: Laminate countertops are fabricated with seams, so clean up spills immediately and avoid flooding water on the surface. Never rest hot cookware or cut food on a laminate countertop.

  Cleaning: Use gentle, nonabrasive, nonacidic cleaners (warm water and dish soap will usually suffice). For stains, use rubbing alcohol or acetone on a clean, soft cloth. Clean in a swirling motion and finish by rinsing with clean water until all cleaner has been removed. Stubborn stains can be removed with a paste of water and baking soda, lightly applied to the surface and then removed with a moistened clean cloth.

- **Granite:** Although an incredibly durable stone, granite does require care and maintenance when used as a countertop.

  Care: Sealing is a confusing issue affecting granite surfaces. How the granite was sealed in the first place will determine whether you need to reseal it on a regular basis. However, any sealant needs to be protected to prevent the surface from becoming unattractively dull. The installer, manufacturer, or retailer will provide sealer instructions. Follow them to keep the counters looking as good as possible. Avoid setting hot cookware on the surface or cutting directly on granite counters.

Cleaning: Clean up spills immediately to avoid staining. For the same reason, don't leave drinks or bottles on the counter. Clean the surface with a cleaner formulated for use on granite surfaces. Avoid vinegar, ammonia, or citrus cleaning agents, and dish soap.

- **Solid-surface composites:** Less expensive than most stone surfaces and as attractive, solid-surface counters are an extremely popular choice among homeowners.

  Care: Wipe up spills immediately. Don't set hot cookware on the surface and use trivets or similar bases for heat-generating appliances like a toaster oven. Don't cut food directly on a solid-surface countertop.

  Cleaning: Clean the surface with ammonia-based sudsy cleansers or any formulated specifically for solid-surface counters.

- **Wood and butcher block:** Butcher block is a long-standing countertop favorite for its country and casual look and feel and a surface that's close to indestructible.

  Care: Unless the surface has been finished or waxed, butcher block should be regularly cleaned, disinfected, and oiled. Use raw linseed oil or food-grade mineral oil. Avoid setting anything that could burn the wood down on the surface, and use a cutting block rather than the counter. Butcher block can stain, so clean up spills immediately and avoid setting wine or other staining food or liquids on the surface. Many people, though, consider signs of age and use part of the charm of butcher block.

Cleaning: Never use abrasive cleansers or scrubbers. Clean with warm water and mild dish soap. In preparation for oiling, clean thoroughly and spray with a half-and-half mixture of white vinegar and water. If needed, scrub out stains with a paste made of water and salt.

- **Quartz:** These countertops are formed of crushed quartz stone in a resin media, creating a look similar to granite. Quartz surfaces are not quite as durable as stone countertops but are resistant to damage if properly cared for.

  Care: Don't use harsh or abrasive cleansers or scouring pads. Don't chop on the surface. Avoid contact with chemicals such as nail polish remover or bleach, inks, or any highly alkaline materials. Don't set hot cookware or appliances directly on a quartz surface.

  Cleaning: Use a mild solution of warm water and detergent to clean a quartz surface. Ideally, use a commercial cleaner formulated for quartz surfaces.

- **Marble:** A marble countertop has a particular opulence all its own. But as hard and enduring as the material can be, it is also susceptible to staining and other damage. In particular, anything acidic is marble's enemy.

  Care: First and foremost, marble counters are sealed and must be resealed regularly. Follow the manufacturer's recommendations. Although the material can tolerate heat, it's wise to use a pad under hot cookware. Don't cut food directly on the surface. Most of all, never let even mildly acidic substances, such as citrus juices, wine, coffee, sodas, or tomatoes, sit on the counter. Wipe up spills right away.

Cleaning: For daily cleaning, a solution of mild dish soap and warm water will work fine (go light on the soap). For regular thorough cleanings (weekly or biweekly), use a cleaner meant specifically for marble countertops.

- **Ceramic tile:** Ceramic tiles are not the favorite they once were for kitchen and bath countertops, but they still offer a variety of sizes, colors, and surface textures at attractive prices. The ceramic itself is easy to care for and clean; the weak spots of any tile countertop are the grout lines.

  Care: Avoid dropping heavy, hard items onto the counter because a broken tile can be an involved repair. Reseal the grout lines yearly to prevent them from stains and grime buildup. You can safely cut on tile and set hot cookware on the surface.

  Cleaning: Clean daily with dish soap and hot water. Clean weekly with a disinfecting cleaner, such as a mild diluted bleach solution, or a half-and-half mixture of hot water and vinegar. Grout lines are best revived with a deep cleaning using a soft toothbrush and a commercial grout cleaner and sanitizer.

- **Stainless steel:** Used in many restaurants, stainless steel is easy to clean and maintain, but the look and feel are a little cold for home kitchens. That's why stainless steel is best used sparingly, such as to top a kitchen island.

  Care: You can set hot cookware on stainless steel and even cut food on the surface, although most homeowners find it too noisy for chopping and some techniques can scratch the surfaces. Avoid dropping heavy items on the counter because it can dent.

  Cleaning: Stainless steel is easy to clean, even though smudges and fingerprints show readily. Use a solution of mild dish soap and hot water and a clean cloth, wiping in a circular motion. Sanitize after foods like raw chicken or pork with a mild solution of bleach and warm water.

- **Others:** Although the options above are the most popular and common, you may have opted for something more unusual in your house. Recycled paper, volcanic rock, concrete, and recycled glass countertops all have their own weaknesses and care and cleaning requirements. Follow the guidance provided by the installer, seller, or manufacturer.

Install a Laminate Floor

TIME: 8 hours (for a basic room) / **SKILL LEVEL:** Moderate

Laminate flooring is a fantastic option for the inexperienced DIYer who would be overwhelmed by the prospect of installing and finishing a new wood floor but who wants the satisfaction and cost savings of self-installation. Simply put, the floor is created by laminating layers on top of a fiberboard base, including a photo layer bonded and covered with a protective clear coating. Today's laminates are significantly more durable and scratch resistant than earlier versions. You can choose surface appearances ranging from common softwoods and exotic hardwoods to stones and even colorful tile versions. All are installed with a simple click-and-lock process that requires few tools and even less expertise. If you are installing laminate in laundry rooms or bathrooms, look for products specifically labeled as water- or moisture-resistant. All types are appealing, warm, and comfortable underfoot. Laminates can theoretically be installed over just about any stable existing floor other than carpet but are ideally placed on a clean and level subfloor. When estimating flooring, measure the square footage and add 10 percent for waste (remember to add closet floors).

What You'll Need

- **Laminate flooring and underlayment**
- **Pry bar**
- **Gloves**
- **Safety glasses**
- **Kneepads**
- **Level**
- **Liquid floor leveler (optional)**
- **Tape measure**
- **Carpenter's pencil**
- **6-mil plastic sheeting**
- **Wood shims or spacers**
- **Circular saw**
- **Miter saw**
- **Tapping block**
- **Rubber mallet**
- **Pencil compass**
- **Pull bar**
- **Hammer**
- **Jigsaw (optional)**

How You Do It

1. Pry off any baseboards and store in a safe location. Cut and remove any carpet, and pry up carpet tack strips. Remove any loose or damaged floor. Check your manufacturer's information to determine if you can lay the laminate over the existing surface.

2. Inspect a subfloor or existing floor for nail heads, screw points, or other obstructions. Remove any you find. Check for level all across the floor and use floor leveler, if needed, to level any low areas, following the directions on the pail.

3. Measure the floor's width (the boards will run perpendicular to this direction). Subtract ³/₄" for expansion and contraction. Divide that number by the width of a laminate plank (without tongue). This is the number of rows. If it leaves a partial board width, rip boards in the first row to this width. (If the remaining is less than half a plank, rip boards for the first and last rows to half the leftover amount to create a balanced appearance).

4. If you're installing on concrete, tape down a 6-mil plastic vapor barrier to cover the floor and use vinyl tape to cover the overlaps and seams at the edges. In any case, roll out the underlayment supplied with the flooring you've purchased. Follow the instructions for installing it. It's usually unrolled; cut to fit with a utility knife, with each row being taped or stuck together. *Optional:* Some manufacturers supply ³/₈" plastic spacers. If not, you can easily cut your own from wood shims. The spacers save you time and effort when installing boards at the edges of the room. Place them every 6" around the walls bordering the floor.

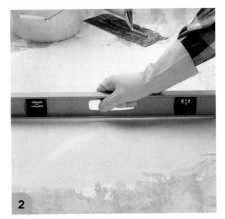

5. Open the boxes and check the flooring for flawed pieces. Lay out the first two rows to determine where boards will follow and avoid awkwardly duplicating patterns.

6. Use a circular saw to rip the starter row boards as necessary, cutting the waste on the tongue edge of the board. If the boards in the first row don't need to be ripped, cut off the tongues.

7. Measure, mark, and crosscut one-third off the end of a plank using the miter saw. These two pieces will start the second and third rows respectively, to stagger the seams.

8. Lay the first row along the wall, starting with a full plank. Align the end tongue and grooves for each successive piece. For the last plank, crosscut it to fit as necessary in the corner, maintaining the ³/₈" gap at the wall.

(continued) ▶

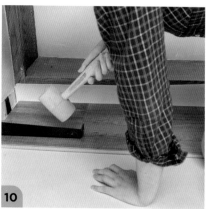

9. Add rows starting each with a full, two-thirds, or one-third plank successively. Fit each plank into the row before by slipping the new plank's tongue into the groove of the previous row and snapping the board into place. If necessary, use a tapping block and rubber mallet to tap the end or groove side of boards to lock them into position.

10. Cut the last plank in each row to fit and use a pull bar and rubber mallet to pull it into place on the end of the row.

11. For the last row, lay each edge plank on the row before it, using a scrap plank vertically as a spacer against the wall. Scribe the cut line on the face of the edge plank with a pencil compass following the wall contour. Use a circular saw or jigsaw to cut the plank along the scribed line.

12. Install final row planks by slipping the tongue into the previous row's groove. Use a pull bar and a hammer to fully seat the edge planks in place. Reinstall baseboard and trim.

Modify Laminate Flooring for Obstacles

TIME: 30 minutes (per alteration) / **SKILL LEVEL:** Moderate

Inevitably, you'll have to accommodate pipes, floor vents, and other obstacles when laying laminate flooring. Precise measurements are key to doing this seamlessly.

What You'll Need

- Pencil
- Tape measure
- Metal straightedge
- Hole saw
- Clamps
- Power drill and bits
- Jigsaw

How You Do It

1. For pipes, align the plank in position against the pipe and mark the pipe location on the plank edge. Measure in the distance from the wall and pipe, adding ³⁄₈" for the expansion gap. Use a hole saw one size larger than the pipe's diameter to create a hole. Clamp it over a sacrificial piece and cut the hole from the bottom of the board.

2. Make two cuts to create channel from the edge to the hole. Place the plank.

3. For floor vents, measure the outline and transfer the measurements to the top of the plank. Drill a corner access hole and use a jigsaw to cut out the vent opening in the plank.

Fix a Squeaking Floor

TIME: 30 minutes / **SKILL LEVEL:** Easy

Flooring sits on a subfloor. In most homes, the subfloor rests on joists that can be accessed in a crawl space or basement. (The ceiling must be opened to implement these solutions for a second story floor.) Although getting to the area can be a challenge, the actual fixes are simple.

What You'll Need

- Flashlight
- Wood shims
- Tape measure
- Utility knife
- Hammer
- 2×6 blocking
- Miter or table saw
- Construction adhesive
- Caulk gun
- Power drill and bits
- 3" wood screws
- ¾" wood screws

How You Do It

1. Locate the squeaking spot as precisely as possible, by using a flashlight to check the subfloor while a helper walks across the floor. Any obvious subfloor movement will usually be a trouble spot.

2. In areas where there is flexing, shim between the joist and subfloor by cutting shims to fit with a utility knife and tapping them in place with a hammer. Test the floor again to check that this has resolved the problem.

3. If older, undersized joists are moving when the floor is walked on, install blocking between the joists to stabilize them. Measure, cut, and screw the blocking and lay a bead of construction adhesive along the top before positioning it. Screw the joists on each side to blocking with the blocking held flush to the subfloor. Use 3" wood screws.

4. If the squeaking is caused by a floorboard that has come loose of the subfloor, face-screwing it would mar the surface. Instead, drive a ¾" screw from below to secure wood, laminate, or engineered wood flooring to the subfloor. (Make absolutely sure before you do that the screw will not penetrate the flooring top surface.)

Repair a Deep Wood Floor Scratch

TIME: 20 minutes / **SKILL LEVEL:** Easy

All it takes is trying to move a large piece of furniture without a sliding pad, and suddenly your beautiful wood floor is marred with a deep scratch. A modest quick fix is all that's needed to restore the appearance.

What You'll Need

- Dust mask
- Random orbital sander
- 160-grit sandpaper (or finer)
- Putty knife
- Non-wax wood filler
- Rubber gloves
- 1" brush
- Wood stain
- Polyurethane or other finish

How You Do It

1. Wear a dust mask and use the random orbital sander with a fine-grit sandpaper to sand the scratched boards down to bare wood. *Pro Tip:* Sand the length of each board in its entirety to better blend the repair into the entire floor.

2. Use a putty knife to fill the scratch with non-wax wood filler (tinted versions will match the floor more exactly). Let the filler dry, then sand smooth.

3. Using a brush equal to the width of a floor board, stain the sanded boards as needed to match the surrounding floor. Let dry and finish with a top coat that matches the rest of the floor.

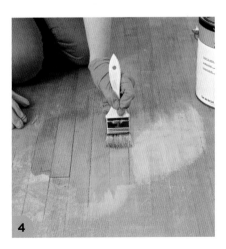

Replace a Damaged Laminate Plank

TIME: 45 minutes / **SKILL LEVEL:** Moderate

As wonderful as laminate floors are, they are more susceptible to damage than wood or stone tile. Fortunately, wholesale replacement of a damaged laminate plank isn't difficult.

What You'll Need

- Wood chisel
- Pry bar
- Replacement laminate plank
- Finish nails
- Hammer
- Nailset

How You Do It

1. Remove any molding covering the edge of the plank nearest the wall, on the side closest to the damaged plank. Use a chisel or pry bar, and try to keep the molding intact for reuse.

2. Use a pry bar to pry the plank closest to the wall up and out. Continue removing planks until you reach the damaged plank. Remove it.

3. Snap the replacement plank into position and replace the planks you removed. Reinstall the moldings and use a nailset to sink the nail heads. Cover the nail heads with wood putty and finish or paint as needed to blend.

Replace Cracked Floor Tile

TIME: 2 hours / **SKILL LEVEL:** Challenging

Ceramic and stone floor tiles are durable and attractive, but it is possible to break one. It's just a matter of dropping something heavy at a certain angle, and you'll have an unsightly cracked tile in the middle of a floor. This project focuses on floor tile, but the same process can be used to replace a cracked or chipped wall tile (less often a problem, but just as unsightly). Aside from the obvious negative appearance, a cracked tile allows water infiltration that can quickly cause damage to a subfloor and beyond. Depending on how severe the crack is, it might even present a tripping hazard. For those reasons—and the look of your floor—replace a cracked tile as soon as you notice it.

What You'll Need

- Kneepads
- Replacement tile
- Grout saw or utility knife
- Small cold chisel
- Hammer
- Putty knife
- Sponge
- Bucket
- Premixed thinset mortar (preferably acrylic)
- Mortar trowel
- Torpedo level or straightedge
- Small grout float
- Premixed grout

How You Do It

1. Have the replacement tile on hand before you start removing the broken tile. This may take some searching if you or the previous owner did not set aside extra tile when the floor was laid.

2. Use a grout saw to clean out the grout from all around the broken tile (some DIYers find a utility knife works more effectively for this, but it's easy to snap off the blade). You can also use a utility knife to cut the seal around the edges of the broken tile and then remove wider grout lines with the grout saw.

Pro Tip

Depending on the floor's age, matching old tile can be a big challenge. Rather than checking at a home center, head right to a tile store. Not only will the selection be greater, the pros in the store are more likely to be able to help you find an exact match, even if they don't have it in the store.

(continued) ▶

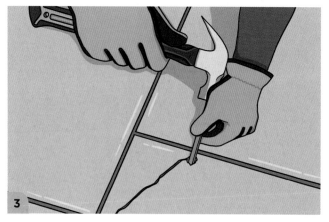

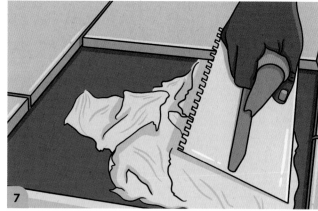

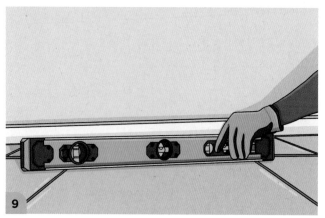

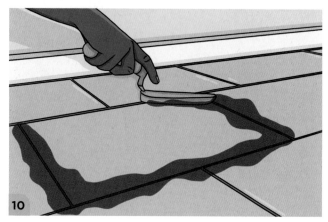

3. Use a chisel and hammer to work under the cracked area and start prying out pieces of the broken tile. Be very careful not to impact the grout lines or otherwise damage the intact tiles surrounding the broken tile.

4. If the grout bed around the edges of the broken tile fractures and comes loose, remove it for better access. Carefully remove the rest of the broken tile.

5. Remove all the old, dried mortar under the broken tile. Use a putty knife or other implement to pry up stubborn portions. Clean the area to wind up as close to bare wood subfloor as possible.

6. Use a moistened sponge to clean up dust left behind, and slightly moisten the subfloor so that it doesn't dry the new mastic too quickly.

7. Use a small notched knife to spread acrylic mortar over the subfloor in the tile space. Use the unnotched side of a mortar trowel to spread the mortar in an even layer. Then use the notched side to furrow the mortar bed.

8. Immediately set the new tile in the mortar bed, leaving an even amount of space between the new tile and the existing tiles around it. Press down on the tile and wiggle it back and forth to ensure a good bond with the mastic.

9. Use a torpedo level or straightedge to check that the new tile is level with the tiles all around it. Clean off any residual mortar on the surface and let it dry completely. Do not walk on the tile in the meantime.

10. Use a small trowel or mini float to force premixed grout into the joints around the new tile. To make the grout blend in better, buy a pre-tinted grout that matches the existing grout shade as closely as possible. Finish the joints with a grout finishing tool.

11. Scrape up clumps of grout with a putty knife and clean the surface with a moist sponge. Wipe over the new grout joints diagonally, being careful not pull any grout out of the joints. When the surface is clean, leave the grout to cure for 24 hours, making sure no one walks on the tile. Once the grout is completely cured, wash and dry the floor and buff the new tile surface with a soft, dry cloth.

6. Exterior Concerns

The outside of a house requires as much maintenance as the inside does. And while the homeowner is the only one who has to tolerate problems on the interior, exterior issues affect curb appeal and neighbors' attitudes and can even impact house association rules. What's more, exterior problems can lead to damage to the structure of the house.

Exterior maintenance includes both the protective surfaces on your home and related areas like walkways, driveways, and garages or sheds. Some of these, such as foundation walls and roof soffit vents, can have a profound effect on the interior when they are compromised. The roof, however, is the area most subject to problems because it has to endure the most direct exposure to the elements and toler ate shifting in the structure itself. Roofing and gutters degrade over time. Keeping an eye on those is part of what should be an annual, if not semiannual, exterior inspection. It is especially important to catch any problems with the roof early before they cause greater damage that could result in the need for a new roof—an incredibly expensive proposition.

A house's exterior walls are all constructed of similar layers. For wood, vinyl, metal, or composite siding, the framed walls are—from the inside out—insulated, sheathed with plywood, covered with building wrap or felt paper, and then sided (left). The process is only slightly different for applied siding such as stucco (right), which is laid on a layer of metal lath that has been nailed to the building wrap and sheathing.

●●○

Locate Roof Leaks

TIME: 20 minutes / **SKILL LEVEL:** Moderate

Finding a roof leak is half the battle to fixing the problem. That's because it's not always clear where the water is coming in. Water wicks and follows the path of least resistance, which means wherever you detect the leak and subsequent damage may be far from the actual hole in the roof. The steps here will help you track down the source of any roof leak.

What You'll Need

- Ladder
- Flashlight
- Awl or power drill with small bit
- Bucket
- Tape measure

How You Do It

1. In the attic, examine the underside of the roof sheathing with a flashlight during a rainstorm or while a helper sprays the roof with a hose. (This assumes an unfinished space. You may need to remove drywall in a finished attic.) The trail of moisture should be fairly obvious; track it back to where it's coming in.

2. Minimize water damage to existing ceilings while you fix the roof. With an awl or drill, make a small hole where water is pooling above a ceiling, and put a bucket underneath it to drain the water.

3. Measure from the leak in the attic, to a feature that will be identifiable outside, such as the peak of the roof. On the roof, use the measurement to locate exactly where the damage is and fix it.

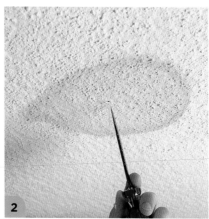

● ● ○

Make Emergency Roof Repairs

TIME: 20 minutes / **SKILL LEVEL:** Moderate

Emergency roof repairs are exactly that—stopgap fixes made in the heat of the moment to prevent near-catastrophic damage from getting even worse. These techniques are most often used when extreme weather damages a roof and you need to immediately prevent the interior from flooding. If you have the time and opportunity—or can get a pro out to deal with the situation—it is always better to make permanent repairs.

What You'll Need

- Ladder
- Fall arrest gear
- Plywood scrap
- Hammer
- Double-headed nails
- 1" × 2" lath or similar
- 6-mil or heavier plastic sheeting or plastic tarp

How You Do It

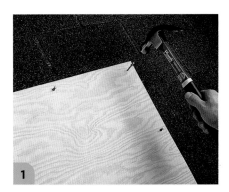

1. The worst-case scenario repair is a piece of plywood nailed directly over a gaping roof hole. This is just meant to hold until the weather event passes and proper repairs can be made. Nail the plywood directly into joists, not just to the roof sheathing, or it may blow off. If possible, use double-headed nails, which will be much easier to remove when you're ready to make a more comprehensive repair.

2. If you don't have plywood on hand, use a frame of 1" × 2" lath to nail down thick plastic sheeting or tarp. As with the plywood, nail the lath (or any long scrap piece of lumber, including 2×4s) directly to the joists. Make sure the plastic is taut.

Safe at Home

Working on any roof entails the danger of falling. Even if you're performing a brief inspection or simple repair, always secure yourself to the roof with fall arrest gear. These vary from leashed harnesses to simple leash-and-safety belts, but all are physically attached to the roof.

Replace Damaged Asphalt Shingles

TIME: 1 hour / **SKILL LEVEL:** Moderate

Although many inexperienced homeowners panic when they see damaged asphalt shingles—thinking the entire roof needs replacing—this is actually a fairly easy repair project.

What You'll Need

- Ladder
- Fall arrest gear
- Heavy-duty work gloves
- Pry bar or claw hammer
- Hammer
- Roofing paper
- Caulk gun
- Roofing cement

How You Do It

1. Pull out the damaged shingles, starting with the highest shingles and working down. Work carefully to avoid damaging surrounding shingles.

2. Remove old nails in and above the repair with a pry bar or claw hammer. Patch damaged felt paper with new roofing paper cut for the patch and fastened in position with roofing cement.

3. Starting with the lowest replacement shingles, nail them in place. Drive 1" roofing nails above the tab slots.

4. Slip the final shingle under the overlapping shingles. Lift the shingles right above the new shingles and nail the top replacement in place.

Work with Flashing

TIME: 30 minutes / **SKILL LEVEL:** Moderate

Flashing is made of galvanized sheet metal, aluminum, or, in some rare cases, copper (other acceptable materials like stainless steel are too expensive for common usage). Crafted into thin sheets, flashing is easy to fabricate with basic tools and little expertise. The main skills you need are cutting and bending the metal to different angles to suit various applications. Whenever you're working with flashing, always wear heavy-duty cut-proof gloves.

What You'll Need

- Flashing
- Tin snips
- Heavy-duty gloves
- Marker
- Locking pliers or clamps
- Scrap 2×6
- Scrap 2×4

How You Do It

1. Cut new flashing with tin snips, using the old piece as a template. This is especially useful for reproducing complicated flashing, such as that around chimneys and dormers.

2. Bend flashing with a jig. There are lots of ways to make a jig, but the easiest is the best. A 2×6 clamped to a work surface on edge is one of the simplest. Slide a piece of flashing up to the bend point that has been marked with a marker and clamp it in place with locking pliers or clamps. Bend along the marked line using a wood block cut from a 2×4 scrap.

●●○

Replace Step Flashing

TIME: 1 hour / **SKILL LEVEL:** Moderate

The flashing most prone to failure is step flashing. It is the protective metal layer between the roof and square or rectangular structures that project out of the roof, like a dormer or a brick chimney. This is a common source of leaks; replacing damaged step flashing has to be done correctly to head off future problems.

What You'll Need

- Ladder
- Fall arrest gear
- Tin snips
- 2×4 (for use as a bending jig)
- Pliers
- Pry bar
- Flashing
- Tape measure
- Marker
- Roofing patch
- Caulk gun
- Hammer
- Roofing nail
- Utility knife
- Nails or screws

How You Do It

1. Bend up any counter flashing or siding covering the damaged flashing. Cut any seams sealed with roofing cement and carefully pull up the shingles overlapping the flashing. Use a pry bar to remove the damaged flashing. Buy replacement flashing to match. *Pro Tip:* Do not use aluminum flashing to flash a chimney or other masonry surface. The mortar will corrode the aluminum.

2. Measure and mark the bend lines on the flashing with a marker, using the old flashing as a template. Use tin snips and a jig to cut and bend the new flashing to match the old, grabbing it with pliers. Apply roofing patch to the mating surfaces. Slip the new flashing in place so that it is overlapped by the shingle higher on the roof and overlaps the flashing below.

3. Nail the new flashing to the roof deck with a single roofing nail. Lay the shingles back down into place and seal all flashing joints with a generous amount of roofing patch. Cut shingles with a utility knife to ensure a proper fit.

● ○ ○

Patch a Steel Gutter

TIME: 30 minutes / **SKILL LEVEL:** Easy

There is a reason that most house gutters today are made of vinyl. That reason is rust. No matter how good a metal gutter was when installed, inevitably, it will rust. The quick fix is to patch the gutter.

What You'll Need

- Ladder
- Heavy-duty work gloves
- Stiff wire brush or steel wool
- Rag
- Roofing cement
- Flashing
- Tin snips
- Tape measure
- Marker
- Bending jig
- Putty knife

How You Do It

1. Scrub the entire area around and over the rotted section, using a wire brush or steel wool. Rinse the surface with water and dry with an old rag. Lay down a layer of roofing cement about $\frac{1}{8}$" to $\frac{1}{4}$" thick, covering the damaged area and a few inches more on all sides.

2. Measure, mark, cut, and bend a piece of flashing to fit over the damaged area, using a bending jig. Press the flashing down into the bed of cement and feather out the edges with a putty knife to prevent damming water flow.

Repair Leaky Metal Downspout Joints

TIME: 30 minutes / **SKILL LEVEL:** Easy

Downspout connections are weak points in any gutter system but particularly with metal gutters. Fix the problem at the first sign of leakage to head off even worse conditions.

What You'll Need

- Heavy-duty work gloves
- Power drill and bits
- Wire brush or steel wool
- Exterior-grade silicone sealant
- Sheet metal screws

How You Do It

1. Drill out rivets or unscrew screws to disassemble the problem joint. Scrub the parts and especially the connection area with a wire brush or steel wool. Clean off the area with water and allow the sections to dry completely before continuing.

2. Lay a bead of exterior-grade silicone sealant around the joints and reassemble the L neck and downspout. Secure the connection with sheet metal screws.

1

2

Upgrade to Vinyl Gutters

TIME: 2 hours (for average house) / **SKILL LEVEL:** Easy

Snap-together vinyl gutters are simple to install and an ideal replacement for metal gutters that have passed their expiration date. The system requires no special tools or skills; the only mechanical fasteners are screw-in hangers. However, gutters of any sort require precise measurements and in-depth planning. Think it through and double-check all measurements and you'll wind up with a professional-looking gutter installation that will go a long way toward keeping the house safe from water infiltration.

What You'll Need

- Vinyl gutter components
- Ladder
- Carpenter's pencil
- Tape measure
- Hammer
- Brads
- Chalk line
- Power drill and bits
- 1 ¼" deck screws
- Hacksaw

How You Do It

1. Mark a point at the high end of each gutter run, 1" down from the drip edge, or top of the fascia. Mark at the opposite end, allowing for ¼" drop per 10' of gutter. Drive brads at the two points and snap a chalk line. For gutter runs longer than 35', mark the slope from the center, down to each end.

2. Screw downspout outlets to the fascia at the ends of the runs you just marked (at least one downspout per 35' of gutter). Align the top of the outlet flush with the chalk line and the edge with the end cap on the house.

continued ▶

3. Screw gutter hangers to the fascia, aligned with the chalk line, every 24". Use 1 1/4" deck screws.

4. Screw inside and outside corner caps for the gutter, at any corner that isn't fitted with outlets.

5. Measure, mark, and use a hacksaw to cut gutter sections to run between corners and outlets. Attach end caps and connect the gutter sections to the outlets. Measure, mark, cut and dry fit gutter sections to fit between outlets, allowing 1/16" to 1/8" at each joint for expansion.

6. Connect gutter sections on the ground before installing them, using supplied connectors. Attach the gutter hangers to the gutter sections and hang them on the support clips you installed.

7. Measure, mark, and use a hacksaw to cut a length of drainpipe to fit between two downspout elbows. One elbow will be connected to the outlet and the other will be secured to the wall of the house. Snap the parts together, secure the elbow in the outlet, and fasten the opposite elbow to the wall with a drainpipe hanger.

8. Measure, mark, and use a hacksaw to cut a length of drainpipe to run from the wall elbow down to end of the drainpipe (which should terminate at least 12" above the ground). Attach an elbow to the drain pipe end and secure it in place with drainpipe hangers. Measure, mark, and cut a final drainpipe section as needed to route water away from the foundation and include a splash block as necessary.

Tune Up a Garage Door

TIME: 30 minutes / **SKILL LEVEL:** Easy

Timely maintenance ensures that your garage door opens and closes at the push of a button, just as it should. This is also a chance to check safety features before you really need them.

What You'll Need

- Scrap 2×4
- Ladder
- Phillips screwdriver
- Batteries
- Lightbulbs (optional)

How You Do It

1. Test the door-opening safety features. Disconnect the opener so that the door can be operated manually. Raise the door about 3' from the ground and let go. If it slams shut, it's unbalanced. Have a professional balance it.

2. Reconnect the opener and place a 2×4 across the garage door threshold. Engage the opener to close the door. As soon as it contacts the board, it should reverse. Do the same test, but this time wave your hand or another object in front of the photocell sensors on either side of the opening. The door should reverse when the connection between the two is interrupted. If these tests point to a malfunction, contact a professional garage door repairperson.

3. Check the battery backup by unplugging the garage door opener and using the car or wall control to open the door. If the door doesn't open, replace the backup batteries. This usually entails unscrewing a cover on the central unit to access the backup batteries. Replace the bulbs in the opener with matching bulbs and the batteries in opener remotes at the same time.

Safe at Home

Garage door cables and springs are kept under high tension. Loosening a cable or spring can result in serious injury and should only be done by professionals. Garage doors are also remarkably heavy. If you're doing work with one in the open position, clamp a C-clamp onto each roller track to ensure the door doesn't accidently fall.

Adjust Garage Door and Track Position

TIME: 30 minutes / **SKILL LEVEL:** Easy

Binding is one of the most common garage door problems. Track misalignment is usually to blame. The process of realigning tracks and the garage door is one of trial and error but will lead to smooth, quiet operation that increases the door opener longevity.

What You'll Need

- Tape measure
- Box wrenches or crescent wrench
- White lithium grease spray
- Rag

How You Do It

1. Close the garage door. Check the gap alongside each edge. It should be uniform—normally ½" to ¾" between door edge and track. Use a wrench to loosen the lag screw on one bracket and adjust the position of the bracket to move the track. Repeat with the other brackets as necessary until the track is aligned with the door edge.

2. Spray white lithium grease into the seam between the hinge bracket and the pin collar on each door hinge. Spray the lubricant into the roller bearings (or roller axle if there are no bearings) on the door rollers. Clean up any overspray with a rag.

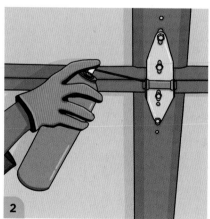

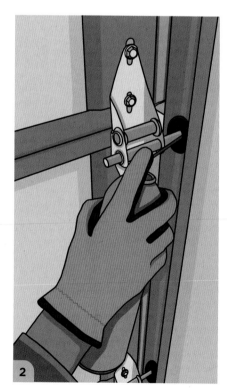

Repair Foundation Wall Cracks

TIME: 45 minutes / **SKILL LEVEL:** Moderate

Foundation walls are subject to cracking as the ground and structure shift over time. A significant crack presents an avenue for water to leak into a basement or crawl space and leads to conditions such as rot or mold. Deal with a crack from the inside.

What You'll Need

- Flashlight (optional)
- Chisel
- Hammer
- Wire brush
- Expanding spray foam
- Hydraulic cement
- Bucket
- Trowel

How You Do It

1. Be sure the crack is stable and hasn't undermined the entire foundation wall or structure. Chisel out a "keyhole" cut, larger at the bottom than at the top. The cavity should wind up no more than ½" deep. Clean out loose debris with a wire brush.

2. Carefully fill the crack with expanding insulating foam, working from the bottom to the top.

3. For larger cracks, mix a small batch of hydraulic cement in a bucket, following the instructions on the bag. Use a small trowel to fill the crack. Apply the cement in thin layers until it is built up slightly above the surface of the wall, then feather it into the surrounding surface. Let dry.

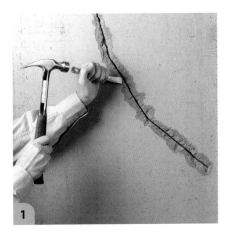

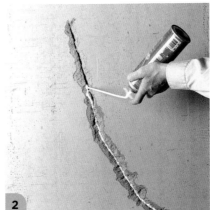

White Flag

If there are multiple large cracks in a foundation or basement wall, or if the planes of the crack are misaligned, you likely won't be able to rectify the situation. But it does need rectifying. Contact a foundation contractor who has relationships with structural engineers. Those professionals will be able to assess the situation and recommend an ideal solution to prevent further structural damage.

Install a Foundation French Drain

TIME: 3 hours / **SKILL LEVEL:** Easy

Natural drainage around a house is rarely ideal. Water should efficiently drain away from the structure and especially the foundation. Standing water can easily infiltrate a basement or crawl space, leading to many serious problems. Water pooling around structures like fences or gazebos can quickly undermine those structures. There is a simple, permanent solution to most drainage problems, and it's called a French drain. It requires little expertise but a lot of hard labor. That's a small price to pay to protect the home foundation or other critical features in the yard or landscape.

What You'll Need

- Tape measure
- Work gloves
- Landscape paint or lime (optional)
- Garden spade or shovel
- Landscape fabric
- Coarse gravel or landscaping stone
- 4" perforated pipe, or 4" PVC pipe
- 4" × 4" × 6' board or similar tamper
- Power drill and bits (optional)
- Steel rake
- Sod or ground cover (optional)
- Sod roller

How You Do It

1. Decide where you want to direct runoff water. Ideally, it should be funneled to a curb or a place in your landscape that can absorb runoff. Do not direct water onto a neighbor's property. *Optional:* If you're installing a French drain for an area other than the house foundation, mark the trench borders with landscape paint or lime.

2. Remove and preserve any sod covering the trench location. Dig a trench at least 18" deep and 1' wide. (If you're installing the drain along a full-height basement wall with significant water pooling, the trench can be as deep as 4' to effectively drain excess water.) The trench must slope 1" for every 10', in the direction you want the water to drain.

3. Line the trench with landscape fabric or other permeable filtering fabric. The fabric should run up the sides about 6" to 8" above the trench lip on either side. Add 3" of gravel or landscaping stone to create a drainage bed. If the gravel is fine, tamp it down.

4. Lay perforated pipe along the gravel bed (this is sometimes sold as "drain tile"). Cover the pipe with gravel and fold the extra landscape fabric over the top of the gravel.

Optional: For a more durable solution in a straight trench, or where the trench is deeper, use 4" PVC pipe instead of perforated pipe. Drill ⅛" holes every 4" to 6" all along and around the pipe before laying it in the trench.

5. Replace the soil in the trench and tamp down with a 4" × 4" board or similar tamper. Moisten the soil, rake the top, and lay the preserved sod over the soil (or replace with new sod or ground cover). Roll it with a sod roller or similar to seat the sod.

Safe at Home

Call the local utility before installing a French drain to determine the location of any underground wires or pipes. Local utility companies will come out and mark the location of any underground

Stop Deck Sway

TIME: 1 hour / **SKILL LEVEL:** Challenging

There are few things as unsettling as having your elevated deck start swaying. Remedy the problem immediately to prevent structural damage or injury. It's important to note that this repair should only be made to an otherwise sound deck. If the problem is part of a large rot problem or the consequence of a poorly built deck, rebuild the deck. This project requires a helper.

What You'll Need

- Tape measure
- Carpenter's pencil
- Band saw or miter saw
- Power drill and bits
- 6" lag screws and washers
- Carriage bolts (optional)

How You Do It

1. Measure down 24" from where a corner post intersects a beam. Mark that spot with a carpenter's pencil.

2. Measure and mark 24" out from the face of the post along both sides of the beam. Measure diagonally from these marks down to the post mark and add 4"; this is the length of the brace. Cut the brace with a band saw or a miter saw, making multiple cuts (or have it cut to length at a home center or lumberyard). The brace should be the same stock as the post. Current codes call for 6" × 6" posts. *Note:* Local codes may call for a different technique to mount the beam on top of the post than is shown here.

3. Have a helper hold the brace in place diagonally between the marks on the post and the beam so that the marks are right in the middle of the brace. Use the post edge and beam bottom edge to mark the brace for the angled cuts. Cut the beam or have it cut at a lumberyard.

4. Have a helper hold the brace in position and drill two countersunk pilot holes at each end for the lag screws (top).

5. Fasten the brace to the beam and post with 6" lag screws. If you have to fasten the brace between two sides of a sandwich beam as shown here, drill through the both sides and the brace and secure the brace with carriage bolts.

Remedy a Spongy Deck

TIME: 90 minutes / **SKILL LEVEL:** Moderate

If the deck seems to be springy or soft underfoot, take these simple steps to ensure structural integrity.

What You'll Need

- Tape measure
- Circular saw
- 2" × 6" lumber
- Ladder
- Hammer
- Penny nails
- Chalk line
- 3" deck screws
- Power drill and bits

How You Do It

1. Measure the space between the joists. This should be standardized and is usually 16" on center, although some builders use 12" spacing for greater strength. Measure between each joist pair, because settling may have caused slight differences in spacing. Use a circular saw to cut blocking to go between the joists, from 2" × 6" lumber.

2. Measure and mark the center of the joists on either side of the deck. Hammer a penny nail at those points and use them to anchor a chalk line, running across the centers of all the joints. Snap the chalk line to mark the joists.

3. Tap the blocking into the space between the joists so that alternating blocks are on opposite sides of the chalk line.

4. Drive 3" galvanized deck screws through the face of each joist into the ends of the blocking. Use three screws per end.

●●○

Patch a Hole in Concrete

TIME: 45 minutes / **SKILL LEVEL:** Moderate

Unless it has been laid correctly and given exactly the right amount of time to cure, a concrete surface will eventually be subjected to degradation. Small and large holes can be the result of physical damage or "spaulding" over time, a process in which pieces of the concrete fracture and break off. A permanent fix is a matter of providing a clean bed for the patch.

What You'll Need

- Work gloves
- Straightedge
- Marker
- Circular saw with masonry blade
- 1× scrap board
- Chisel
- Hammer
- Wire brush
- Sand-mix concrete with acrylic fortifier
- Trowel
- Concrete float
- 6-mil plastic sheeting

How You Do It

1. Mark straight cut lines around the damaged area. Cut along the lines using a circular saw with a masonry blade. Set the blade to cut away from the center at a 15° angle, and make the cut with the saw's shoe riding on a 1× scrap board.

2. Chisel out the damaged area down to rough aggregate. This gives the new patch a good surface on which to bond. Clean out any loose debris with a wire brush.

3. Prepare sand-mix concrete with acrylic fortifier, and use a trowel to cover the damaged patch just slightly higher than the surrounding area.

4. Use a float to smooth and feather the patch into the surrounding surface. Re-create any surface effect, such as broom strokes. Cover with plastic sheeting and protect from foot traffic for at least 48 hours.

Repair Concrete Cracks

TIME: 45 minutes / **SKILL LEVEL:** Moderate

Concrete walls, walkways, and driveways all have a tendency to crack over time because the ground is constantly shifting and concrete isn't very flexible. The solution for a given concrete crack depends on the size and location of the damage.

SIZE	SURFACE	PATCH
<$\frac{1}{4}$" wide	Vertical	Concrete caulk (temporary solution)
>$\frac{1}{4}$" wide	Vertical	Vinyl-reinforced concrete or hydraulic cement
<$\frac{1}{2}$" wide	Horizontal	Vinyl-reinforced concrete patching compound
>$\frac{1}{2}$" wide	Horizontal	Fortified sand-mix concrete

What You'll Need

- Wire brush
- Power drill with wire wheel attachment (optional)
- Stone chisel
- Hammer
- Latex bonding agent
- 1" to 2" paintbrush
- Vinyl-reinforced patching compound
- Trowel
- 6-mil plastic sheeting
- Sand-mix concrete with acrylic fortifier (optional)

How You Do It

1. Clean out loose debris from the crack using a wire brush. For larger cracks, use a power drill with a wire wheel attachment.

2. Prepare the crack for filling by chiseling it out to create a keyhole cut (wider at the bottom than the top). Clean out any remaining debris with the wire brush.

3. Thoroughly coat the crack with latex bonding agent using a 1" to 2" paintbrush. Mix a small batch of vinyl-reinforced patching compound and trowel it into the crack. Feather the surface with the trowel to level it flush with the surrounding area and blend the edges. Cover a horizontal surface with plastic sheeting and protect it from foot traffic for 7 days. *Optional:* For larger, deeper cracks on horizontal surfaces, prepare as above, but then pour sand into the crack to within $\frac{1}{2}$" of the surface. Make a small batch of sand-mix concrete and add a fortifier. Trowel the concrete into the crack, leveling the top to match the surrounding surface and feathering the edges to blend.

Pro Tip

There's a reason you'll find so many concrete products on the home center shelf. Each has its own best application. When it comes to patching concrete holes, for instance, size matters. Smaller holes less than ½" deep are best filled with a vinyl-reinforced concrete patch product. For deeper holes and cracks, use a sand-mix concrete fortified with acrylic or latex. In both cases, follow the manufacturer's mixing and application directions for best results.

Yearly Maintenance Calendar

This calendar is meant as a foundation for customizing your own. Change frequency or season of a given listing (such as replacing a furnace filter) depending on where you live, how many people live in the house, and your own preferences.

January

- Replace furnace filter.
- Replace batteries in all home remotes, including ceiling fans and garage door openers.
- Test smoke and carbon monoxide detectors; replace the backup batteries.
- Drain water heater water and sediment.
- Inspect home fire extinguishers.
- Test GFCI receptacles.

February

- Test smoke and carbon monoxide detectors.
- Inspect home fire extinguishers.
- Test garage door auto-reverse functions.
- Test GFCI receptacles.

March

- Test smoke and carbon monoxide detectors.
- Replace furnace filter.
- Inspect home fire extinguishers
- Test GFCI receptacles.

April

- Clean gutters.
- Test smoke and carbon monoxide detectors.
- Inspect home fire extinguishers.
- Reverse ceiling fan direction.
- Test GFCI receptacles.
- Have septic system inspected by a professional.
- Clean faucet aerators in all faucets.
- Clean showerheads with vinegar or scum-removing cleanser.

May

- Replace furnace filter.
- Test smoke and carbon monoxide detectors.
- Clean air-conditioning condensers and clean or replace filters.
- Inspect home fire extinguishers.
- Test garage door auto-reverse functions.
- Test GFCI receptacles.

June

- Clean windows and repair or replace damaged screens.
- Test smoke and carbon monoxide detectors.
- Clean refrigerator coils and condenser.
- Inspect home fire extinguishers.
- Test GFCI receptacles.
- Check the water heater anode for wear.

July

- Replace furnace filter.
- Test smoke and carbon monoxide detectors.
- Inspect home fire extinguishers.
- Test GFCI receptacles.

August

- Inspect caulked joints around doors and windows and replace worn caulk.
- Test smoke and carbon monoxide detectors.
- Inspect home fire extinguishers.
- Test GFCI receptacles.
- Test water-main shutoff valve.

September

- Replace furnace filter.
- Patch concrete walkways and seal asphalt driveways.
- Test smoke and carbon monoxide detectors.
- Inspect roof for missing or damaged shingles and flashing, and repair or replace as necessary.
- Check weather stripping around doors and windows and replace any that is failing.
- Change the ceiling fan direction.
- Inspect home fire extinguishers.
- Test GFCI receptacles.
- Clean faucet aerators in all faucets.
- Clean showerheads with vinegar or scum-removing cleanser.

October

- Have professional clean fireplace chimney.
- Test smoke and carbon monoxide detectors.
- Test basement sump pump, if any.
- Inspect home fire extinguishers.
- Test GFCI receptacles.
- Turn off water supply to exterior hose bibs to prevent freezing. Open those faucets to drain all water out of the pipe.

November

- Replace furnace filter.
- Test smoke and carbon monoxide detectors.
- Inspect home fire extinguishers.
- Test garage door auto-reverse functions.
- Test GFCI receptacles.

December

- Test smoke and carbon monoxide detectors.
- Clean gutters.
- Inspect home fire extinguishers.
- Test GFCI receptacles.

Conversion Chart

CONVERTING MEASUREMENTS

TO CONVERT:	TO:	MULTIPLY BY:
Inches	Millimeters	25.4
Inches	Centimeters	2.54
Feet	Meters	0.305
Yards	Meters	0.914
Square inches	Square centimeters	6.45
Square feet	Square meters	0.093
Square yards	Square meters	0.836
Cubic inches	Cubic centimeters	16.4
Cubic feet	Cubic meters	0.0283
Cubic yards	Cubic meters	0.765
Pounds	Kilograms	0.454

TO CONVERT:	TO:	MULTIPLY BY:
Millimeters	Inches	0.039
Centimeters	Inches	0.394
Meters	Feet	3.28
Meters	Yards	1.09
Square centimeters	Square inches	0.155
Square meters	Square feet	10.8
Square meters	Square yards	1.2
Cubic centimeters	Cubic inches	0.061
Cubic meters	Cubic feet	35.3
Cubic meters	Cubic yards	1.31
Kilograms	Pounds	2.2

COUNTERBORE, SHANK & PILOT HOLE DIAMETERS

SCREW SIZE	COUNTERBORE DIAMETER FOR SCREW HEAD (IN INCHES)	CLEARANCE HOLE FOR SCREW SHANK (IN INCHES)	PILOT HOLE DIAMETER	
			HARD WOOD (IN INCHES)	SOFT WOOD (IN INCHES)
#1	.146 ($9/64$)	$5/64$	$3/64$	$1/32$
#2	$1/4$	$3/32$	$3/64$	$1/32$
#3	$1/4$	$7/64$	$1/16$	$3/64$
#4	$1/4$	$1/8$	$1/16$	$3/64$
#5	$1/4$	$1/8$	$5/64$	$1/16$
#6	$5/16$	$9/64$	$3/32$	$5/64$
#7	$5/16$	$5/32$	$3/32$	$5/64$
#8	$3/8$	$11/64$	$1/8$	$3/32$
#9	$3/8$	$11/64$	$1/8$	$3/32$
#10	$3/8$	$3/16$	$1/8$	$7/64$
#11	$1/2$	$3/16$	$5/32$	$9/64$
#12	$1/2$	$7/32$	$9/64$	$1/8$

LUMBER DIMENSIONS

NOMINAL - U.S.	ACTUAL - U.S. (IN INCHES)	METRIC
1 × 2	¾ × 1½	19 × 38 mm
1 × 3	¾ × 2½	19 × 64 mm
1 × 4	¾ × 3½	19 × 89 mm
1 × 5	¾ × 4½	19 × 114 mm
1 × 6	¾ × 5½	19 × 140 mm
1 × 7	¾ × 6¼	19 × 159 mm
1 × 8	¾ × 7¼	19 × 184 mm
1 × 10	¾ × 9¼	19 × 235 mm
1 × 12	¾ × 11¼	19 × 286 mm
1¼ × 4	1 × 3½	25 × 89 mm
1¼ × 6	1 × 5½	25 × 140 mm
1¼ × 8	1 × 7¼	25 × 184 mm
1¼ × 10	1 × 9¼	25 × 235 mm
1¼ × 12	1 × 11¼	25 × 286 mm
1½ × 4	1¼ × 3½	32 × 89 mm
1½ × 6	1¼ × 5½	32 × 140 mm
1½ × 8	1¼ × 7¼	32 × 184 mm
1½ × 10	1¼ × 9¼	32 × 235 mm
1½ × 12	1¼ × 11¼	32 × 286 mm
2 × 4	1½ × 3½	38 × 89 mm
2 × 6	1½ × 5½	38 × 140 mm
2 × 8	1½ × 7¼	38 × 184 mm
2 × 10	1½ × 9¼	38 × 235 mm
2 × 12	1½ × 11¼	38 × 286 mm
3 × 6	2½ × 5½	64 × 140 mm
4 × 4	3½ × 3½	89 × 89 mm
4 × 6	3½ × 5½	89 × 140 mm

NAILS

Nail lengths are identified by numbers from 4 to 60 followed by the letter "d," which stands for "penny." For general framing and repair work, use common or box nails. Common nails are best suited to framing work where strength is important. Box nails are smaller in diameter than common nails, which makes them easier to drive and less likely to split wood. Use box nails for light work and thin materials. Most common and box nails have a cement or vinyl coating that improves their holding power.

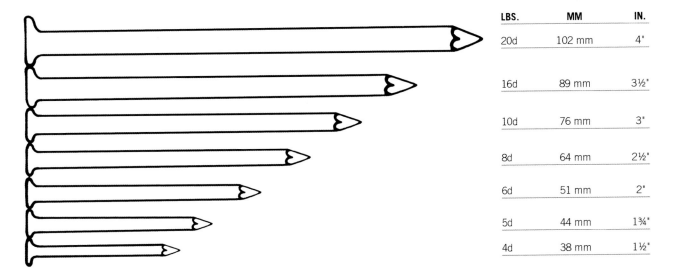

LBS.	MM	IN.
20d	102 mm	4"
16d	89 mm	3½"
10d	76 mm	3"
8d	64 mm	2½"
6d	51 mm	2"
5d	44 mm	1¾"
4d	38 mm	1½"

Resources

Black + Decker
Tools, project instructions, and more
www.blackanddecker.com

Chimney Safety Institute of America
Advice and information about chimney maintenance, safety, and more
www.csia.org/homeowners.html

Forest Stewardship Council
Information on sustainable wood products for the home
www.us.fsc.org

National Association of Home Builders (NAHB)
Basic home maintenance and repair information for homeowners
www.nahb.org

National Kitchen and Bath Association (NKBA)
Industry association offering remodeling advice and connection to qualified experts
www.nkba.org

National Roofing Contractors Association (NRCA)
Offers a consumer section with listings for contractors and in-depth information on roofing
www.nrca.net

U.S. Department of Energy
Guidance on conserving energy, choosing home energy options, and saving on energy bills
www.energy.gov/energysaver/energy-saver

Photo Credits
[LIST PHOTO CREDITS HERE]

Index